BLUE STAR IN MY WINDOW

**By
Catherine DePew**

2007

Copyright © 2007 by Catherine DePew

Blue Star In My Window
by Catherine DePew

Printed in the United States of America

ISBN 978-1-60477-281-4

All rights reserved solely by the author. The author guarantees all contents are original and do not infringe upon the legal rights of any other person or work. No part of this book may be reproduced in any form without the permission of the author. The views expressed in this book are not necessarily those of the publisher.

Unless otherwise indicated, Bible quotations are taken from the *Holy Bible*, New International Version. Copyright © 1973, 1978, 1984 by International Bible Society.

www.xulonpress.com

TABLE OF CONTENTS

History of Blue Flag
Dedication
Forward
Introduction

When I first began my
    diary, June 23, 2007
March 10, 2007, 7:00 a.m.

August 23, 2004, Evening/
    January 2007

NOVEMBER 2004
November 6, 2004
November 12, 2004
November 13, 2004

Much time passed

Introductions

Home Team & Away
    Team
The dream

Parris Island Recruit

Blissfield train ride

Mary, how did you do it?

MAY 2005
May 28, 2005
May 31, 2005

JUNE 2005
June 28, 2005, 4:30 a.m.

JULY 2005
July 14, 2005, 5:50 a.m.
July 18, 2005
July 19, 2005   1759 service
                                 member deaths
July 24, 2005
July 29, 2005

AUGUST 2005
August 4, 2005
August 5, 2005
August 6, 2005   14 from Ohio
August 6, 2005   Pen pals
August 6, 2005, Later in   No news is good
   the day   news
August 15, 2005   Atta boy stuff
August 19, 2005   Mom, where did you
                                    go?
August 22, 2005, 7:15 a.m.
August 23, 2005, 5:07 a.m.   Tatoos
August 30, 2005
August 30, 2005, 1:25 a.m.
August 31, 2005, 5:00 p.m.   Check lists

August 31, 2005, 9:45 p.m.

SEPTEMBER 2005
September 1, 2005, 3:00 a.m.

The mothers of America have ruined the Corps!
September 6, 2005

September 6, 2005
September 7, 2005, 9:35 a.m.
September 8, 2005, 5:55 p.m.
September 13, 2005, 5:20 a.m.
September 15, 2005, 5:30 a.m.
September 17, 2005, 8:00 p.m.
September 20, 2005, 6:30 a.m.
Abba, Father, Dad, Pops, My ol' man

Don't do drugs, Mom
Detroit Metro

Good Gravy

The man I want to be

1902 service member deaths

OCTOBER 2005
October 22, 2005
October 24, 2005
October 25, 2005

Overpass Artist

2000 service members

NOVEMBER 2005
November 4, 2005

November 6, 2005	Grouchy Mom
November 8, 2005	
November 9, 2005	
November 17, 2005	
November 18, 2005	
November 24, 2005	Thanksgiving Day
November 26, 2005	
November 28, 2005, 11:25 p.m.	

DECEMBER 2005

December 2, 2005	
December 12, 2005, 2:36 a.m.	Lessons to learn
December 14, 2005, 1:35 a.m.	
December 14, 2005, 11:20 a.m.	Joy!
December 16, 2005	
December 19, 2005, 4:35 a.m.	Fear not
December 23, 2005, 9:50 p.m.	
December 25, 2005, 12:15 p.m.	Christmas with the troops
December 26, 2005	

JANUARY 2006

January 2, 2006
January 6, 2006, 12:30 p.m.

January 7, 2006, 6:45 a.m./ January 7, 2006, 8:50 p.m.	
January 8, 2006, 11:55 a.m.	Faded Flag
January 9, 2006, 9:28 a.m.	Brave heroes of the 2/6
January 12, 2006, 3:45 p.m.	
January 13, 2006, 7:30 a.m.	An archer's arrow
January 15, 2006	
January 18, 2006, 7:30 p.m.	2236 service members
January 20, 2006, 3:15 a.m.	Judge of the Earth
January 22, 2006, 7:00 p.m.	
January 25, 2006	
January 29, 2006, 5:30 a.m.	Marine Moms
January 30, 2006, Noon	

FEBRUARY 2006

February 4, 2006, 5:30 p.m.	Big Ben/Big Ken
February 5, 2006, 6:15 a.m.	
February 7, 2006, 9:35 p.m.	Danish cartoon
February 8, 2006, 8:30 p.m.	
February 12, 2006, 8:25 a.m.	
February 18, 2006, 7:30 a.m.	
February 21, 2006, 1:00 p.m.	
February 21, 2006, 3:03 a.m.	
February 22, 2006, 8:00 p.m.	

February 22, 2006, 10:00 p.m.	Two kids
February 23, 2006, 8:00 p.m.	Religion versus Faith/2286
February 24, 2006, 6:00 a.m.	Proverbs 24:6
February 26, 2006	
February 26, 2006, 8:30 p.m.	
February 27, 2006, 9:00 a.m.	

MARCH 2006
March 3, 2006, 7:00 a.m.	
March 5, 2006, 9:30 p.m.	Connect the dots
March 13, 2006, 9:00 p.m.	War hug
March 14, 2006	
March 14, 2006	Micah 6:8
March 16, 2006, Evening	Gunny in the black truck
March 30, 2006, 8:30 p.m.	Amazing Grace

APRIL 2006
April 1, 2006, 6:30 a.m.	
April 8, 2006, 5:00 a.m.	
April 13, 2006, 7:30 a.m.	
April 14, 2006, 10:30 p.m.	Norman Rockwell
April 15, 2006, 10:00 a.m./10:00 p.m.	Sand in my hands
April 21, 2006, 4:00 a.m.	
April 2006	Weekend Homecoming

April 27, 2006   Remember Me
April 28, 2006, 10:00 a.m. Cigs and cones
April 28, 2006, 9:00 p.m.

MAY 2006
May 1, 2006   Mrs. Gust's class
May 2, 2006, 5:00 a.m.
May 5, 2006, 5:30 p.m.   Oil and Water
May 6, 2006, 5:45 a.m.
May 11, 2006
May 22, 2006, 10:20 p.m.
Memorial Day 2006   David's Mighty Men

AUGUST 2006
August 7, 2006   The way it is
August 22, 2006   Prodigals

OCTOBER 2006
October 1, 2006   Class of Post 9/11

FEBRUARY 2007
February 4, 2007, 4:30 p.m. Aunt Lill's afghan
February 4, 2007, Later in Laundry room
  the day   lesson
July 15, 2007   Muted Sacrifice
May 24, 2007   Poppy

AN INVITATION

HISTORY OF THE BLUE STAR SERVICE BANNER

Army Captain Robert L. Queissner of the 5th Ohio Infantry designed and patented the Blue Star Service Banner in 1917 while serving in World War I. He had two sons serving during World War I and sought to honor their service. During World War II, the United States government formalized specifications for the Blue Star Service Banner. The blue star signifies a member of the family currently on active duty in military service. The banner can have up to five stars. If a service member dies or is killed while in the service of the country, a smaller gold star is placed upon the blue star in order that a blue border outlines the gold star.

Our blue star hangs in the front window of our home honoring the service of our son. Many military families proudly display the Blue Star Service Banner to honor their son(s) or daughter(s). Take a drive through your neighborhood or town. I'll just bet you see one!

PSALM 46

God is our refuge and strength,
An ever-present help in trouble.
Therefore we will not fear, though the earth give way
And the mountains fall into the heart of the sea,
Though its waters roar and foam
And the mountains quake with their surging.
Selah

There is a river whose streams make glad the City of God,
The holy place where the Most High dwells.
God is within her, she will not fall;
God will help her at break of day.
Nations are in uproar, kingdoms fall;
He lifts his voice, the earth melts.

The LORD Almighty is with us;
The God of Jacob is our fortress.
Selah

Come and see the works of the LORD,
The desolations he has brought on the earth.
He makes the wars cease to the ends of the earth;
He breaks the bow and shatters the spear,
He burns the shields with fire.
"Be still, and know that I am God;
I will be exalted among the nations,
I will be exalted in the earth."

The LORD Almighty is with us;
The God of Jacob is our fortress.
Selah

DEDICATION

This story is dedicated to the memory of the brave heroes who have fallen in this Iraq war, as well as those in Afghanistan. As of this writing, the number stands at approximately 3789 precious lives. Several fallen heroes forever touched my son's life from the 2/6. And this is dedicated with a special salute to three United States Marines of the 2/6 Echo Company who sacrificed their all on January 7, 2006, in Fallujah, Iraq: PFC Kyle Brown, LCpl. Jeriad Jacobs, and Cpl. Brett Lundstrom and their beloved families. Semper Fi.

You will never be forgotten.

Psalm 44:25, 26 "We are brought down to the dust; our bodies cling to the ground. Rise up and help us; redeem us because of Your unfailing love."

Psalm 49:15 "But God will redeem my life from the grave; He will surely take me to Himself." Selah

FORWARD

When people hear about deployments of troops, they think about the service members and what they might experience while "in harms way." In the backs of our minds, we remember that they all have families whether they are single or married. The news media does a story once in a while about a wife or child or parent. Rarely do we get to look deep inside the heart and mind of a family member for any length of time. Catherine DePew has given us that rare look.

It isn't that other mothers and fathers, husbands, wives or children have not had similar thoughts. It is, I think, that most of us would not have the courage to write those thoughts down. You see, to write them down is to make them too real. If I only think them, then maybe they won't come true—maybe I won't feel so helpless.

I have known Cathy DePew since college days, but I came to know her better immediately after college when we shared an upstairs apartment in an old Victorian home along with another college friend. No matter what we went through, Cathy had an infectious laugh. She was straightforward and dependable. Even today she is as I have always known her.

Her faith has been formed in a lifetime of trusting God even through the long- term illness and death of her first husband, Kurt Dial. I was not surprised that her diary from her son's deployment would be open, honest, and utterly transparent. I was even less surprised that she would draw important spiritual lessons from each day. She has put herself out there for all of us who might be too afraid to write our thoughts down or go on this terrifying journey. She has served us well. I suspect that there will be many a mother and father, husband and wife, son or daughter who might resonate with her words. The details of their stories might be different, but the journey is so similar.

It is the spiritual journey that Cathy most wants to share. She is not ashamed of this Hope she has. It is not childish, wishful thinking. It is based on a faith that she has put to the test many times and that faith has grown in depth and breadth. "Now faith is being sure of what we hope for and certain of what we do not see." (Hebrews 11:1, New International Version) Cathy could only risk writing down her life with such naked honesty because she lives with a certainty about the future.

Read her words and listen in on her thoughts and conversations with God. Be gentle and gracious to her. Do not judge her—after all, you are being allowed to walk on holy ground. Let her struggles inform you of the Hope that is in the journey with you. You are not alone. But I warn you that what is here is raw and real.

If you are not a military family member, then perhaps you will get a better picture of what others wrestle with at night when things are much too quiet or in the day when even busyness won't keep the numbness at bay. Perhaps you will know better what it means to sacrifice for one's country. Whatever the case, you will be richer for having traveled this private, sacred journey. Thank you, Cathy, for letting us come along.

Karen J. Diefendorf
Chaplain (Lieutenant Colonel) U. S. Army, retired

INTRODUCTION

When I first began my diary, I had no idea where it would take me. I'm thankful I kept writing. I'm thankful for I times I wrote these thoughts down because in the busyness and business of life, I would have forgotten so much.

I'm thankful first to my God. He has literally been my song in the night. He has comforted me through His living Word in many dark nights and days. There have been times when *only* after reading the scriptures that I have finally been able to sleep peacefully. There have been times when I opened to a passage that spoke to me so personally of my current situation that I knew it was God's Spirit drawing me to that particular passage.

> ***"Do not be anxious about anything, but in everything, by prayer and petition, with thanksgiving, present your requests to God. And the peace of God, which transcends all***

understanding, will guard your hearts and your minds in Christ Jesus." Philippians 4:6, 7

God has been my Abba Father. He has been there for me. And I am eternally grateful to Him most of all.

I'm thankful for my good family. We're not rich, famous, or beautiful. We're simply an American family—like so many families—who have been touched by this Iraq war. We love our children and want the best for them. We are proud of the ones who go off to serve their country voluntarily. Their extraordinary courage, honor, and commitment are an inspiration to us in our ordinary lives. I'm thankful to have met so many wonderful families that support their troops. Moms and Dads, wives and husbands, sisters and brothers who stay at home and quietly fight the war in their homes. For these families, the war is never far away…it follows us to our dinner tables over the evening news and bedrooms as we awaken in the dark to wonder how our loved ones are doing on the other side of the moon. It creeps in at noontime while we're on our lunch breaks. It stops us as we pass a newsstand and see a violent picture of destruction on the front page. It follows our children to school on the playgrounds in their recess and homerooms during conversations of current events. These children of warriors and sisters and brothers of the troops…they carry the war inside their young lives as well. We write letters, send care packages, fly our flags, pray, and talk. Some of us agree. Some of us disagree. It doesn't change the fact that we love and support our troops.

I'm thankful for the veterans of foreign wars. So many have said, "God bless your son." "We're praying for him." "Tell him thank you for us." They truly understand. They are the ones who have been there; and sometimes the tears in their softening eyes speak volumes that I could never express in print. Thank you, dear veteran, for your service to our country. My love and thankfulness goes out to them as well.

It is my prayer that something in these writings will encourage or lift you, the reader, to a higher level. As I said above, I am a private person. It is difficult to release some of these very personal memories. But my son has told me, "Go for it." This is his story and our family's story...we are but one small voice in the loud din of public opinion over this war which has brought division to our country. My goal is to point people to God and to His Son, Jesus Christ. For it is in Him, that I have life and the courage to face whatever the future may hold. So it can be for you.

So erase us out of the story and see where God may lead you, dear reader. My prayer is that this points you to Him and His living Word. History is His Story from Genesis to Revelation and back again...past, present, and future.

Catherine DePew
Proud Marine Mom
June 23, 2007

March 10, 2007   7:00 a.m.

We are ordinary families. Nothing special. We live on your street. We go to work each day. We are truck drivers, farmers, teachers. Some of us work in the court systems or own restaurants. We deliver your newspaper or work in corporate America. We might be a construction worker or an architect. Some of us go to college and some don't. Some of us are small and are still in the arms of our mothers or sit in a school room each weekday. We see you at the grocery store or wait on you in the mall. We are all around you. We are the family members of the U.S. military. Ordinary people with an extraordinary job. We support our sons and daughters, husbands and wives, brothers and sisters, Moms and Dads in the job they do.

We don't know their bosses or always understand their chain of command. We can go for months without seeing our loved ones. However, rarely a moment goes by that they're not in our thoughts. We whisper prayers for them in the quietness of our cars. In the middle of the night when the phone rings, we pull ourselves out of the thick fog of sleep and snap to attention when we hear their voice on the other end of the line. We check our in box for emails from them or tap off a quick Motomail of news from home. We collect information from other families in support groups; and we pack care boxes with white socks, gum, batteries, magazines, and Oreos. We watch the news shows and scan the faces on the screen for our loved ones. We sign get well cards for the injured and send sympathy cards with heavy hearts to those dear families who have paid such a high price for our freedoms.

Many of us hold our opinions inside ourselves. And some of us voice them loudly. We answer your questions without giving away too much information. We see the signs of protest. We watch the politicians debate. We agree. We disagree. We snap shut our brains sometimes because it is too much. Endless words. Unknown endings. Decisions pending. Tears and frustrations well up when we see the pictures. Innocent, bleeding children lying on foreign muddy streets. Mothers and fathers with hands raised in grief and rage for lost loved ones. Men carrying more coffins. Dismemberment and death 24/7. Our sons and daughters, our husbands and wives in a foreign land who have responded to the call of our nation. A nation of divided opinion polls. Short attention spans that dart from celebrity to war policy in the click of 30 minutes on the talk show circuit. We sigh deeply, remember our loved one, and go on. And we pray for God to help us.

This is just one story of one family. We are nothing special as you will see. But we are incredibly blessed by love for one another. We are proud of our young son, the job he does, and for the man he is becoming. We are thankful for the time we've had with him and the lessons of life we've learned from one another. We are a family...now a growing military family with our son's new sweet wife and an expected, adored baby on the way. This is our story of deployment and homecoming: two words that conjure up such a score of different emotions. The home team and the away team. We thank those who supported us during this time and will never forget the many kindnesses extended to our family and our beloved son, a United States Marine.

August 23, 2004   Evening

I had a deep, disturbing dream last night. It was so vivid it bothered me throughout the day.

Our family seemed to be on a vacation. I remember a hotel-type place facing the ocean or a large body of water. Another angle of the glassed in room faced an island-type inlet of water. A terrible storm blew up, and the room we were in broke off—intact—and started to go into the large body of water. We were aware of the breakaway and seemed to see other people on the inlet watching us be separated and tossed into the water. I remember glass windows facing turbulent water; and yet the room seemed to still supply oxygen for life. However, there seemed to be uncertainty for how long the oxygen would last. The waves were large and overpowering. Twice today I have been reminded of Jesus' teaching on building our lives on a firm foundation—not sand.

> *Matthew 7:24-27*
> *Therefore anyone who hears these words of mine and puts them into practice is like a wise man who built his house on the rock. The rain came down, the streams rose, and the winds blew and beat against that house; yet it did*

not fall, because it had its foundation on the rock. But everyone who hears these words of mine and does not put them into practice is like a foolish man who built his house on sand. The rain came down, the streams rose, and the winds blew and beat against that house, and it fell with a great crash.

I pray I've been a wise builder.

I believe in a God who reveals things to his children in dreams. Not just to Joseph or Daniel in ancient times (Daniel 2:24-28). There is a God in heaven who reveals mysteries.

My August 2004 dream came true on several levels. I wonder about the allusion to a physical storm—this dream almost a year to the date of Hurricane Katrina. But I also know of the turbulence 2004 brought when our only son joined the United States Marine Corps during Operation Iraqi Freedom. There have been times when I have gulped for oxygen—if not physically, certainly emotionally and spiritually. The dream was a preparation for what was to come, I believe.

Catherine DePew
January 2007

November 6, 2004

I feel so numb and so sad…and numb…and sad.

It's Saturday of the week Kenton left. He turned our world upside down. Tuesday, November 2, 2004, was also Election Day in the United States. Before I could believe it, Kenton was heading out the door—not once looking back—and into the darkness of the 4:00 a.m. dawn. When I got the call from Lenny telling me of the United States Marine Corps offer to take Kenton into service TONIGHT, my prayers began.

I walked out of the Wildwood Athletic Club and barely remember turning on the truck and driving home on Holland-Sylvania Road. One of the ladies from my aquarobics class later asked me, "Were you all right? You looked so devastated after you got the phone call."

On the 10-minute drive home, I prayed aloud to my heavenly Father: GOD, I MUST HEAR FROM YOU! And in that drive down Holland-Sylvania…I can show you the exact spot, two things became very clear to me.

1. You cannot teach him anymore. You've taught him all you can.
2. I will protect him.

I told Kenton those two things after he had signed his papers to join the United States Marine Corps on our drive home from the recruiter's office that evening. He said it seemed everything was coming together as it should. It was "his birthday, Thanksgiving, and Christmas all rolled into one crazy night," he said.

So now he's gone four days to the Parris Island Marine Corps Recruit Depot. At work I can push the loneliness aside. Being home this weekend has been hard. I miss him—his noise, his comments, his presence. I feel like I'm in grief. I guess maybe I am. I raked leaves. We shopped together today, but it was lonely. I took our dog Joey for a walk late afternoon, and a young man was jogging with his head phones. Even at a distance Joey was fooled; and he got excited thinking it was Kenton running toward us. But it was not.

What in the world is Kenton doing? Is he exhausted, tired out of his brain, scared, excited, confused? Probably all of the above. I pray God gives him the strength for each task the drill instructors bark out. Watch over him, please God, and keep him safe.

Friday, November 12, 2004

What absolute joy a piece of mail can bring. We got our first letter from Recruit Dial today; and it was a good, positive letter. Thank You, God! I've run the gamut this week of real loneliness to almost thinking he's at work at Kroger's and will be home tonight. Not to be, however.

I was so relieved to hear that at least it sounds like he's getting settled in at Parris Island. The book I'm reading, <u>Keeping Faith: A Father / Son Story About Love and the USMC</u>, by Frank Schaeffer has been riveting. Very informative. Sometimes I have to snap it shut because it becomes TOO real. The gas chamber part—the filling out of paperwork indicating where your body should go—too fresh to me now.

On Veteran's Day, a co-worker's husband Paul, came into the office and gave me a strong hug from one Marine to a Recruit Mom. There was a wistful look in his eyes. I've enjoyed writing letters—four so far Tuesday through Friday. I try to encourage Kenton and give him some spiritual food on which to feast. I pray it helps him. I've prayed that God strengthens him from the inside out. *"Train up a child in the say he should go; and when he is old, he will not depart from it."*

That is my hope and prayer.

November 13, 2004   Saturday

I'm just missing him tonight. Two Saturdays have passed, and I miss his energy.

We stopped by for some grocery items tonight, and there was a young boy at Sam's Club—maybe 12 years old—who reminded me of a young Kenton. He was teasing his Dad and being silly. What sweet days—innocent days—those were. He was so eager to please and do it right.

I'm sure Kenton is still trying to please some drill instructor now—to do it right—stay focused. I'm terrified if he fails, what will happen; and I'm terrified if he succeeds, what will happen. To be a Marine in a time of war; it crushes me to think of this now. It's so unsettling.

God, I can only pray for Your hand of protection over my son's life. Watch over him, please, guide and direct his life.

I must not forget Katelyn, our 10 year old daughter, in all of this. We went to Blissfield, Michigan today for a pre-holiday celebration and rode the old train. This was her first train ride. Katelyn was looking out the wooden and glass window, and the sunlight reflected on her beautiful Madonna-like face. The strands of gold glistened in her hair as she faced the large window observing the passing sights in the cold Michigan countryside. Thank You, Lord, for the gifts of BOTH my children.

Amen

~~~~~~

Much time passed between the diary entries of November, 2004 and the next entry of May 28, 2005. Letters between Kenton and me became our way of communication, and I poured my thoughts into these epistles to my son. The 13 weeks of USMC boot camp finally passed, and Family Day and Graduation Day came that last week of January, 2005.

Lenny, Katelyn, and I were joined by Grandma and Grandpa Krouse on the trip to Parris Island, South Carolina. A cold, blue January sky brightened our way from Ohio to the first stop in Tennessee. We spent two nights in Pigeon Forge, Tennessee; and

I couldn't wait to get going to Parris Island. It was Thursday morning when we arrived on Parris Island. I looked at these guardians of my son in a much different manner than I had when we had visited two years prior on a Family Day. We were now part of the family...no longer outsiders.

I remember very clearly seeing Kenton's first USMC picture. I cried. He looked so grown up to me, and I could see so clearly Kurt's outline on his face. "He looks so much like Kurt...I never realized." Kurt, can you see our son? Are you here with us now? Does God allow the curtain to heaven to be drawn back from time to time for heaven's spectators to view earthly milestones? Kurt, I remember one of the last words you spoke was for Kenton. "Be sure he stays with God. Keep him in church." I've tried to honor that, dear father of Kenton. You loved him so. I know you must be aware of what a big deal this entrance into the world of the United States Marine Corps is to your son.

We met another man, an uncle of another new Marine. He was there to stand in the gap for his deceased brother. He had raised his nephew as his son; and in his USMC jacket, he showed all the pride of a Dad for that young man. I thought of my own dear husband, Lenny. He too had stood in the gap for young Kenton when he took on first-time fatherhood of the 8-year old boy. When Lenny and I returned from our 1992 honeymoon, young Kenton bounded out to greet us. "What do I call you? Step-dad or Lenny?" Lenny wisely replied, "There's no 'step' in our family, Kenton. It's either Dad or Lenny." And

Dad it was from that time on. Lenny could have burst his buttons off his winter coat with the pride in his heart that day also.

We watched with the other families as these recruits became the newest members of the USMC. On that frozen morning of January 28, 2005, we families bundled together and cheered, cried, and hugged these young men and women for their proud accomplishment on this Island.

Kenton with his Dad on Parris Island Graduation Day

Mary, how did you do it?

You knew from the time the angel first came to you that you were carrying a special son. One bright, starlit night in a cleaned up stable, he came to you. You kissed his tiny, soft head. You probably hummed to him a sweet song to soothe him to sleep. You treasured all these things in your heart. You and Joseph took him to the temple on his eighth day of earthly life to dedicate him to God. And while there, you learned from Simeon that a sword would pierce your own soul because of him. So you knew somewhere . . . somehow . . . the pain of separation awaited you.

Jesus . . . 12 years old and lost! Where could he be? You searched with relatives, friends for his familiar face . . . dark eyes, dark hair. Where could he have gone to? And when you found him again at the temple, he looked at you in a different way. "Did you not know I was about my Father's business?" Again you were reminded: don't hold onto to him too tightly. Soon he'll go.

Pride in your heart for the fine young man he grew up to be. Sometimes you were able to steal away a few minutes just to talk to him alone. He taught you so much . . . wisdom beyond his earthly years, maturity for the task that lay ahead, a dedication to the One who gave him his name. No fear for what lay ahead.

And on the cross, he continued to look out for you. In one of his last earthly acts, he asked John to take care of you, his mother. And you felt the sting of the sword that pierced your own soul.

Mary, how did you do it?

You knew what was to come. And you did it with praise and a dedication to raising the Son of God entrusted to you.

I look at my son. He's 21. Ready to march off to a war. And my heart is pierced with a sword. I can't imagine the separation, fear, worry I'll feel while he's gone. I can't protect him from the horror he'll see and the job that must be done. When he was a boy, his father and I dedicated him to God. We've watched with pride, amusement, and love to see him grow into this young man who now hears a call to arms. I've treasured all these things in my heart. Yet, he looks at it with a maturity beyond his years for the task that lies ahead.

But, God . . . what if they kill him?

I hear the song of Mary through the ages. They killed her son. And she continued with a song of praise in spite of the sword that pierced her heart. "Hold onto your child lightly. Release him to the Father. In the Father's hands, your child is safe no matter what." Jesus said, "Father, into Your hands I commit my spirit."

I release this Marine son to you, Father. Please give me the grace to hold onto him lightly, and help me to remember *You* hold him in *Your* hands tightly.

~~~~~~~~~~~~~~~~~~~~~~~~~~~~~~~~~~~~~~~

May 28, 2005   Memorial Day weekend

What a beautiful surprise of Kenton's UNEXPECTED homecoming. Seeing him stand before us was a stunning moment. It was hard to comprehend he was HOME. I think I hugged him three times to be sure it wasn't a dream!

Kenton had called the Sunday before from Camp Lejeune, North Carolina saying he needed to borrow some money. He couldn't say why, but could I please send him money quick? I worried that he was in trouble for something. I sent the money and put it behind myself. Little did I know, he had told his grandmother (and no one else) that it was his plan to come home for Memorial Day weekend to surprise us. He arranged all the transportation, and everyone then was in on the secret of his return. I had NO idea! When Kenton got out of the car, our dog Joey went over and sat on his feet. Kenton moved and Joey simply moved over and sat on his feet again. It was Joey's sweet way of saying, "My boy is home, and I will not let him leave again."

He's definitely a Marine in the fleet now. He's passed Parris Island, done School of Infantry at Camp Geiger, and is now in the 2nd Battalion, 6th Marines, Echo Company. He'll go for infantry training at Twentynine Palms, California this summer. Iraq lies ahead in September 2005.

It's funny how last night as I sat on the back porch, I looked at our tree in the backyard. The tree is full and green, just newly filled out from the rains of May. I began thinking of how when Kenton goes, the leaves will be turning their colors and falling again to the ground in their seasonal pattern. And it comes to me: STOP!! Don't rush so through the summer. Enjoy the PRESENT! I do that a lot. Wish away time. And, good grief, what a surprise I had awaiting me. God gave me the present of my son this Memorial Day weekend!

Thank You, Lord!

May 31, 2005

I just finished my third trip into Kenton's bedroom to pick up after his visit. I strip the bed and can smell the young warrior's scent on the sheets. I think that's because he was so busy, he had no time to shower his last night! Receipts from the Charlotte airport terminal, cash withdrawal slips from Camp Lejeune…all signs of his entry into adulthood. Some jolting news also, of which I wish I didn't know. Still, I am glad Kenton has always been open with his Dad and me. He told us he's been drunk in North Carolina. My heart sank of that news. One of the guys with whom I work had told me just last week that I was deceiving myself if I thought Kenton hadn't had alcohol. I said I didn't think so, but I am wrong. He said beer tastes bad, but it makes things "so funny." He told us of throwing up and wanting his bed in Ohio the next morning. His Dad and I shared our disappointment in this revelation, but Lenny said it best and was the most firm—as a Dad should be. He said, we didn't allow this, Kenton knew that, and it wasn't in his family's history to do so.

Last night around midnight, Kenton said, he got scared again thinking of going back. He said the same thing at the airport in Columbus, Ohio the night before he left for School of Infantry. I'm sure the reality of his decision is scary—and so when opportunity arises for "fun" in life, the "boots" grab it. I'm not trying to excuse him, for I truly hope and pray he won't go there again.

Deployment plans are now for Twentynine Palms, California July 20 – August 20, ten days of leave at home, and then onto Iraq. I cringe writing that. I looked at the world map in the downstairs conference room at work and found Syria, Iraq, Iran, and all the other hot spots on the globe. My world is Sylvania/Toledo; and that "other world" is in the newspaper. Now that is all changing. That other world will enter my living room, my bedroom, my dreams, and hopes for my son.

Lenny, Katelyn, and I went to the Memorial Day service yesterday at the local cemetery. Rep. Marcy Kaptur read the names of all the Ohioans who'd died in Iraq. The names went on forever—FAR TOO MANY. The woman standing next to me just shook her head; and I found it hard to keep the tears from rolling. There were just so many Private, PFC, and LCpl. names all indicating those dear, young, brave warriors. I wondered how those families were faring this Memorial Day.

June 28, 2005   4:30 a.m.

I'm reflecting back over this past week of vacation this early morning. It was a good vacation with unusually "good" stuff happening. Sometimes God gives us the grace to stop us in our tracks, make amends, and hopefully move forward in a better way.

We enjoyed Fathers' Day weekend with Kenton at Camp Lejeune, North Carolina. It was eye-opening to be in Kenton's military "jarhead" world, if only ever so briefly. It's a different culture: pecking order—chain of command kind of world. Toughen up the inward as well as the outward.

One thing I'll never forget. I was standing outside Kenton's barracks on the breezy Sunday afternoon awaiting Kenton and Lenny to return. I observed a company of young Marines departing for their "field" operations. At first it startled me to see the young men with their rifles drawn over their shoulders, packing bags of supplies on their backs. It started as a slow trickle of Marines walking toward the beach area where their intended gathering spot was to be. A large, noisy truck would rumble by, another truck gathered supplies for this journey. And then came a pouring of young men marching toward the beach. So many walking down that sandy, grassless beach front. I began to look at the faces of these men—almost childlike faces on some of them in their grown up cammies. These were no toy soldiers though. My mind sees so many young, nameless Marines marching off to yet another drill to prepare for their battles ahead. And my heart says, "They're so young. Look at those faces." I pray for their skills, their protection, and their now gone innocence. I see older, grayer Marines walking alongside these young charges. They to pass the baton to this young bunch of stallions.

My son, while not in this particular march, is in the same way preparing for battle. I am reminded of the young David of the Psalms. I've told Kenton to model himself after this David. He was a mighty warrior, yet his heart was tender always toward God.

I read of the Psalm 144 warrior, yet David's heart was tender always toward God. Psalm 144:1-4

> *Praise be to the LORD my Rock who trains my hands for war, my fingers for battle. He is my loving God and my fortress, my stronghold and my deliverer, my shield, in whom I take refuge, who subdues people under me.*

Please train his hands for this battle, Lord God. Please make him the best assault man he's capable of being. Keep Your hand of protection over his young life, Lord, and those other brave young men and women. Draw this generation close to You, Father. Get their attention in these battles that they might become more mindful of You. Draw them close to You, and never let them go. Keep the enemy far from them, help them uncover evil, and protect the innocent.

Thank You for listening, Lord.

The other vacation event was Monday's fight between Lenny and me. A long, festering wound was torn open. Both Lenny and I had hard words to say.

I cried a long-cleansing cry.
He shouted.
I was angry; he was angry.
I was wrong. He was wrong.
We forgave.
We prayed.
We go on.
Our marriage is better for it.

We're both hard-headed and knuckleheads who take each other for granted. Heal our marriage, Lord, and help us to grow in grace to You and one another.

July 14, 2005   5:50 a.m.

It's 5:50 a.m. My body is tired, but my mind won't allow me to sleep. I had a dumb dream last night. I was 20 minutes late to work in a Hallmark store that I think I was to have opened, and I had to keep stopping to ask directions because I didn't know where the store was. Also, my sister Mickey was in it. She was asking if she could help me; and I asked her to do my towels because they were dirty and needed washing.

Life has been a bit overwhelming lately. I guess it's taking its toll.

Kenton has final inspection today before flying out to California on Sunday. I pray for him. I'm so thankful he is a responsible young man eager to pull his own weight. Proverbs 14:33 is a good verse to remember today: *"Wisdom reposes in the heart of the discerning and even among fools she lets herself be known."* (I try to read the Proverb associated with the current day of that month.)

I need YOUR wisdom, Lord, to deal with life. HELP!!! Please keep me going, Father.

July 18, 2005

Kenton left for Twentynine Palms, California today. His plane left at 1900 hours. I called too late to talk to him as he was told to leave his cell phone behind. It's probably preparation for the distance that's upcoming.

He called me Saturday at work; and we had a good conversation. He said he was fighting the uneasiness that he always feels before a change in venue. He said he felt it before Parris Island, School of Infantry, and the entry into the fleet. I told him—tried to assure him—this was normal. Fear of the unknown. He knows that in his head, yet he still feels this uneasiness.

I told him to remember that he's in the best shape of his life, he's had extensive training, and that the training will kick in when he needs it. And, most importantly, he needed to remember that no matter what: GOD IS IN CONTROL. I told him to anchor down into that reality and know we're all praying for him and are so proud of him. He told me he and others in his group feel like this is the "Mt. Everest" of their young lives. And it absolutely is. He said that they watched a movie of a battalion of Marines who lost 15 of their own. I know he's wondering what will happen in his group—this Echo Company. He'll go over a young kid and come back a changed man. I know that; he knows that. He will pull from these experiences the rest of his life. Our prayers go with these young men and women.

I got off the telephone and the tears came for a brief moment at my desk. Then on with my work. I have to keep going. I have to.

July 19, 2005

U.S. death tolls in **USA Today**: I read these day after day, week after weekday. I zone into the ages, where these young heroes are from. Today ages 24, 22, 21, 34 22, 23. So young…just on the edge of adulthood; and they've sacrificed their all.

They've almost exclusively died from IEDs. Kenton says the insurgents are extremely intelligent and cunning. I'd say. Today on Channel 11, they showed a video of a soldier who'd been shot by an insurgent. He returned fire, injuring the insurgent, then chased the insurgent down, and ended up being his medic—actually helping the man who'd earlier wounded him! Amazing. The only reason they caught it on tape was that the insurgents planned to use it as a "training tape."

1759 service members died so far in Iraq. Who knows how many innocent children and adults in Iraq? Yesterday I grimaced as I saw the picture of a 3-month old infant with its little head bandaged.

So sad.

July 24, 2005

Accomplished a lot today. Sunday I worked—grabbing all the overtime I can get. I feel like our finances are in this deep, sucking hole. No matter how much I work, I can't seem to get caught up. There's never enough money. But beyond that, Pastor's sermon was good. "Work as hard as you can, then step aside, and allow God to work out the details." Well, I have worked hard. Lord, I now ask for your help to finish up what I can't.

Kenton called today—a real bright spot. He said it's so hot in California. The place he's at is very primitive. It's a Quonset hut that he said is like a tin can cut in half that sleeps 25 Marines. The floor, I guess, is sandy. It's beastly hot—in the 100s. Las Vegas was 120 degrees or so today. Kenton said they had 17 heat casualties at training this week. He's doing okay, but there is no air conditioning.

He said he's got a big test Tuesday in which he must do well. He said he didn't hit his targets, but he must hit his targets on Tuesday. I told him I'd pray for him.

He asked if I'd seen a young woman at our church who he thought seemed very nice when he was home on leave in May. I'm praying the heart of God's chosen one for Kenton recognizes his heart, and they find one another in due time. Whomever that young, dear woman may be.

July 29, 2005

Every morning I arise for work: 5:00 a.m. 4:30 a.m. today. I go through the motions of pulling out the makeup and hair tools so I don't look too scary at work! "War paint," Gayle Snell's Dad said. "If the barn needs painting, paint it." said Dr. Wayne Shaw from my alma mater one night at Lincoln Christian College.

I paint my eyes. Methodically putting on the colors, blending, stroking on the mascara. Pull back from the mirror and blink my eyes. Rush off to the day.

Oh, God, open my eyes. Please give me the vision You have. Not just the obvious rush of life-type things. But the insight from Your sight. This ability to see beyond the obvious. Forgive my dullness of heart and sight, Lord. "Open the eyes of my heart, Lord," the song says. "I want to see You, I want to see You." Like the man in Mark 8:21-25. Put Your hands on my eyes and help me to see—beyond the trees—the veiled blur of life. To have the wisdom, discretion, and intuition to hear Your voice, see what You would have me see. I don't want to miss You, Lord, in my hurry. Solomon, in his wisdom, warned about hurrying and missing the way. (*Proverbs 19:2b It is not good . . . to be hasty and miss the way.*) I don't want to miss the God-ordained events, people, situations, in which You teach me. Thank You, Holy Spirit, for writing the Word through people. Thank You, Father, for putting Your thoughts into my hands in Your precious Word, the Holy Bible. Thank You, Jesus, for being God's incarnate Word. I love You so!! Where would I be without You? I need You in my life to carry and sustain me. I thank You for listening, for loving me, for forgiving me, for guiding me. Please mold me into the woman You want me to be. Help me to be the Cathy You desire. The wife, mother, daughter, worker You want me to be.

I love You, Lord, with all my heart. Bless You, Father.

All glory and honor to You above, Lord.

Amen

August 4, 2005

The news bore heartbreaking updates today on 20 Marines' deaths in Iraq. All reservists from outside Cleveland. So sad. Young lives gone forever—6 from a suicide bomber and 14 from an IED. The IED literally flipped the vehicle on its top and those poor 14 never had a chance but to die in a horrible fire. Dear God, where will it end? It seems to be that the enemy is just getting too good. It's so evil. I don't know how they think; it's not like me. Why would you want to blow yourself up? I understand that we are the enemy to them, but young, innocent children—why them?!

Sometimes I feel like I'm going to panic—to melt down. Just the thought of Kenton being in harm's way makes it hard to breathe almost. I wonder what Kenton must be thinking—feeling today upon hearing this devastating news.

This son is so precious to me, God. Please watch over him. Protect him, guide him, and keep him ever close to your heart, God. Keep him ever close to your heart, Lord. I pray the "David's prayer." Make him mighty in battle, Lord, but ever tender toward You, Lord. Guard his heart, Lord. Both my children—keep them ever close to You. Katelyn loves You, Lord. She, too, is so precious to me. Help her young heart to remain tender to You, Father. Thank You for these precious gifts, my children, Lord.

August 5, 2005

There were 14 Marines and one interpreter in a 25-ton amphib van who were on their way to just do their job. Fourteen young Marines sitting in the van, probably exchanging glances one to another as they journeyed on their dangerous trek. They each knew the dangers. The enemy was wise. He was cunning. He knew only too well the paths they were to take.

> Lay low.
> Wait.
> It will only be a matter of time.

Fourteen young Marine lives. A story here. A thought of home there. Plans on hold. Do my job. I've been trained well. Get through another day.

> The enemy waiting
> Scheming
> Hissing his death threats.

One interpreter and fourteen Marines felt the hit. Fifteen lives; fifteen souls. Suddenly a fiery furnace. Oh, Lord, how my heart goes out to these families. The explosion so strong it flipped their 25-ton vehicle on its flat roof like a toy. A fiery furnace in Babylon.

{{

Bow down to me, boys, worship and serve my gods and that image of gold I have set up, Satan screams.

But the boys of Babylon refused. They stood up to the tyranny of the kingship of Nebuchadnezzar whose evil demands went unheeded. Demands of death unless you bow down to my terror, Satan hisses. These three boys—unrelenting—thrown into that fiery furnace made seven times hotter through the King's order. Those soldiers of King Neb even died following the orders of their demanding King. Raving King of destruction. They WILL bow down or die, Daniel 3 tells us!!

{{

These 14 Marines answering the Terror King who demands lives for payment. Thirsty for another's blood – this thirst is never quenched. More death, destruction, I demand. More pain, aching grief, sneers this king of the lower world. Worship me!! Grovel down in my world—my empty image of gold, materialism, terror, hate, and destruction. I have you now, the Snake says.

Fifteen souls in a fiery furnace.

Did they have one brief moment, Lord God, to cry out to You in that terrible time? I believe they did. For it only takes one slim second to cry out, "God, save me!" And You were there in that instant. You're the 16th man: just as the 3 boys of Babylon met You, the 4th Man, in the furnace, I believe those 14 young Marines and one interpreter met You in the fire. You were there for them, Lord. I know that in my heart of hearts, You met and held them in that furnace.

> The enemy gloating in the news of what they had just accomplished.
> Their outstanding defeat in this fiery ordeal.
> We've hit our target, America's finest.

But the enemy is short-sighted and only sees this ending. Father God, You point us beyond this sad story. The souls crying out to You are now with You, Father. They have the best now. You led them Home, Jesus. Again, each day, You show up in Babylon Iraq. You're there at that fiery furnace working each day through those Godly chaplains and other Christians in each confusing circumstance. You're reaching out and calling to each soldier, marine, and civilian heart.

> Come to Me.
> **I am always faithful.**
> I offer eternal life beyond this struggle.

Dear families of these sons of Ohio whom you now grieve, my heart aches for your loss. I can't imagine your pain. May the God of all comfort be with you in your sorrow. Hold them up, Lord, and give them a song in their sorrow. Help them to know that gold and silver emerge from the fire of their Crucible. The tears we shed this day honor these young Marines and the impact their lives have on this generation—a generation who so often only hears the march of the golden image placed beyond them. These 14 Marines and one interpreter, I believe, met the 16th Man—the Son of God—in their furnace, and He walked those who called out to Him Home.

Please, God, turn this tragedy into your glory. May only You be praised. Destroy the enemy of this present world. Help us to hold tight to You, Lord. I pray even for this current enemy. I pray they tire of their crusade, tire of the blood and loss of life, and come even to know You, Lord Jesus. Save their souls.

"Pray for your enemies," Jesus said. I can only do this with kicking and dragging feet. My head tells me I must; my heart is stony to them. But You died for them, too, Jesus. Your words from the cross beckon, "Father, forgive them, for they know not what they do." Holy Spirit, you're going to have to help me with this one. You rescued these 14 Marines because they were precious to you and brought them into your Spacious Place.

    Semper Fi
        Always Faithful
            Rest well, dear sons of Ohio

Based on Daniel 3:1-30

August 6, 2005

I found this letter to President Bush in Katelyn's notebook early this morning.

Dear George W. Bush,

It has been a long time since we talk (sic) to each other. My brother, Kenton, is going to Iraq in September. He is going to miss my birthday. I'm turning 11 (on) September 30. I see you on T.V.

Sincerely,

Katelyn DePew

Adorable! It affects all of us—even little sisters worry.

I sent this to The White House. Katelyn had written the President as an assignment the previous school year, and she'd received a photo of President Bush in the return mail. I guess they're pen pals now!

August 6, 2005   Later in day

Kenton called Saturday from California. It was such a welcome surprise to receive his call. He said Echo is in their last training event Monday through Wednesday this week. They will "role play" Iraq and test Monday through Wednesday. They'll satellite patrol, do close quarter conflict, paintball M16s on Wednesday, vehicle convoys, check points, and assault moves. He said it's so far removed from the feel of the United States—"like Egypt, Mom." It's been 133 degrees. I asked how he stood it, and he said, "I'm past that now." He assured me—at least four times—"I'm well trained, Mom. I'll be okay. If you hear no news for awhile, that's good news." He's been reading Genesis and Exodus—I told him that was good. He would get a lay of the land.

His leave is August 20 – September 7, 2005. Back to Jacksonville, North Carolina and then on to Iraq September 15 or so.

August 15, 2005

Kenton called twice this weekend: Friday and Saturday nights. It means so much to me to know he cares enough to stay in touch. He had just finished their mock "war games" in California. He said several platoons inhabit an actual settlement for urban-type warfare. The houses were 70s style, broken down windows, and each unit practices what they've learned. He said the senior Marine officers were very pleased with their "war readiness." I'm sure they tell all the units that…"atta boy" stuff.

Kenton had a bad case of pink eye affecting his vision in his firing eye. I worry about his eyes and hands, I guess, because of Kurt's issues with them. (Kurt had a congenital birth defect with his left hand that made that hand have only one "finger" and "baby" fingers that never grew. Kurt then lost his eyesight to diabetes 4 years prior to his death—when Kenton was just a year old.) It's irrational, I know, but anytime Kenton mentions a problem, I worry over the smallest thing.

Roberta deBoer from our local newspaper **The Blade** is coming over tonight to go over ground rules for this story she'll write for the local newspaper. What am I doing???! I'm such a blabbermouth! Maybe I should just keep quiet/private things to myself. I guess I'm afraid to probe deeply. Early this morning on Insight For Living, Chuck Swindoll spoke about "the cup" and how each one of us has struggles with the humanity of the cup. If we can get over and through it, great soul-deepening type growth can occur.

I want to be used, O Lord, but it is SO scary. I fluctuate between "I'm fine" modes and nearly given to panic grouchiness. You're going to have to carry this big baby of a mother, Lord!

August 19, 2005   5:30 a.m.

I just finished listening to Insight For Living. Chuck Swindoll inspires me so! I almost think of him in fatherly terms as the kind of wisdom I wished I could have gleaned from my own Dad—had I been able to know him as an adult. Chuck talked about Jesus and the time at the Upper Room where Jesus washed His disciples' feet. "Let me feel the splash of the water and the warmth of the towel," Chuck prayed for all of his listeners. Jesus is the servant Son of God.

Jesus, how I love You. As Max Lucado's book title indicates, "<u>No Wonder They Call Him The Savior</u>." No wonder!! You deserve it all. My heart falls more in love with You each time I hear another story of Your earthly ministry. Keep me focused, Lord God. It's so easy to get bogged down in the day's activities. Currently in my life there are struggles, jealousy in a situation. It's so easy to get caught up in that. To want to talk about the offender, smack him down (which he probably deserves somewhat), and make fun. I wonder what You'd do? Help me to see Your perspective. Help me not to be a doormat. Help me to be your peacemaker.

Kenton comes home tomorrow to start his 17-day leave. I have to set up as much vacation time to be home as I can. Dear, sweet Katelyn has literally begged me to take ½ day vacation for her before school starts again. I must do that today for her. She left me a note that said, "Mom, where did you go?" At 10 years of age, Katelyn says she feels like I've disappeared since I've worked so much this summer. It has been an especially hard work this July/August. I look forward to some much-needed family time, Lord. I pray for a good vacation with Lenny, Katelyn, and Kenton. Bring our family together during these final days before Kenton leaves for Iraq. Help us to realize how special each one of us is to the other, please Lord.

The time with Roberta deBoer went well Wednesday night. The last hour we went over some hard issues. Killing, the morality of it, the guilt that comes, the inner core of a person, and how it affects him. I pray for my dear, tender-hearted son. Again, my "David" prayer: make him mighty in battle, but tender toward You, Father. I know a tender heart is bruised easily. I am concerned about that and how it will affect him. I MUST TRUST that You who created him and his uniqueness will go before him—hem him in before and behind. And bring him into Your maturity. A true crucible—the gold and silver will rise to the top. Proverbs 17:3: *"The crucible for silver and the furnace for gold, but the LORD tests the heart."* Help us, Lord, in this testing time. Holy Spirit, I invite You to go before us, behind us, through us, and lead, guide, and direct. We'll only make it WITH YOU. Thank You for hearing my morning prayer. I love You and bless Your holy name.

August 22, 2005   7:15 a.m.

I just finished watching Charlie Gibson's interview with founding mothers of "Gold Star Families" on Good Morning, America. I came away with tears in my eyes for Ms. Sheehan and Sherwood's mother. Sherwood was a patriot—a noble man who was killed in a "repugnant" war.

I wrestle with all of this. I disagree with protesting the war. I think we're at the tip of public opinion where the tip of the sway will topple over to strong opposition of the war. I hear these mothers' voices, and I want to reach out to them in their grief. Stretch my hands out to them and grasp with no words. A simple touch and prayer saying I'm so sorry for your pain. You have faced what I fear most.

I lay my hand across my mouth because I can't criticize them. Their grief drives them. The anger of loss stokes the fire. I do understand that. But our military sons—they were not/are not little boys. They have become men. They couldn't be "moved to Canada" as you could a 4-year old son, as one of the mothers suggested. THEY made the decision to join the military. And I must honor that adult-made decision as I, too, honor their patriotism, courage, and energy.

My prayers go out to them—these families of the fallen.

August 23, 2005   5:07 a.m.

"Prayer is the urge of the life toward God."

Luke 18:1-8

Then Jesus told his disciples a parable to show them that they should always pray and not give up. He said, "In a certain town there was a judge who neither feared God nor cared about men. And there was a widow in that town who kept coming to him with the plea, "Grant me justice against my adversary."

For some time he refused. But finally he said to himself, "Even though I do not fear God or care about men, yet because this widow keeps bothering me, I will see that she gets justice, so that she won't eventually wear me out with her coming!"

And the Lord said, "Listen to what the unjust judge says. And will not God bring about justice for his chosen ones, who cry out to him day and night? Will he keep putting them off? I tell you, he will see that they get justice, and quickly. However, when the Son of Man comes, will he find faith on earth?"

Kenton got his tattoo USMC on Monday. Lenny and I had a HUGE fight over it. He opposed the tattoo; I said I didn't have a problem with it. (Although I'm not wild about where the tattoo is; I wish it was in an area of his body where it wasn't so prevalent.) Lenny and I made a pact to end the fighting. I called Focus on the Family, and Lenny contacted Perry Stone's organization. I was wrong. There IS a scripture, *Leviticus 19:28, "Do not cut your bodies for the dead or put tattoo marks on yourselves. I am the LORD."*

I HATED being wrong!!! I battle my "stupid superiority" over my husband. He's right on some counts; I'm right on others. We can't allow this to tear us down. Tensions sometimes run high. I'm tired and feel stretched. "Take away this acid that eats away at our soul." Anger...bitterness... The power of persistent prayer. Keep me going, Lord. Thank You for Chuck Swindoll's prayer above.

Sustain me, Lord God. Move me to do Your will. Help me to focus on You and not dwell on myself. Give me HOPE—in You alone. *Proverbs 23:18*

"There is surely a future hope for you, and your hope will not be cut off."

August 30, 2005

Day two of vacation. I'm enjoying thoroughly this slowdown in life. I'm tired; it's all catching up with me, I think. Such a busy, hectic summer. Today was overcast—the approaching tropical depression remnants of Katrina. What a sad, horrific hurricane! So many pitiful stories of helpless people down in the Gulf States. It's VERY sad—so devastating for New Orleans area. I can't even imagine.

Enjoyed activities of today. Went to mall and got a new swimsuit for aqua class. Baked banana bread and watched Oprah and did laundry. Nice afternoon and evening. Roberta deBoer and I had quite an extensive interview Monday. She asked deep, hard questions.

> How do you feel about war?
> Do you think we should be there?
> How do you feel about Cindy Sheehan?
> How does it make you feel to see war protesters?
> Should we try to make it a Christian state?
> Tell me about your faith. When did you "get" it?

I told Roberta about Kurt, and we cried together.
I shared as honestly as I know my faith and beliefs. We talked from 10:30 a.m. to 1:00 p.m. and

the time flew (to me). Enjoyable lunch with Lenny, Roberta, and myself. We then went out to Cathedral of Praise on Strayer Road in Maumee and toured our new building. Kenton will be prayed for on Sunday by the leadership of our church prior to his deployment to Iraq. While Kenton really doesn't want a "big deal," I think it will be special and mean something to him to have the support of our church. Lenny and I shared our vision for a military ministry: the "Rock Room" from Psalm 144.

Kenton, Jimmy, and Doug went to Chicago for a concert in his old green car. He said it was a blast! He brought me a "<u>Purpose Driven</u>" 2006 calendar. He'll be back home in 2006. I washed his cammies and hung them up today. Read a story in **The Wall Street Journal** about quilts for military deceased. Very touching at the end. God bless those quilters for this work and their generosity.

August 30, 2005   1:25 a.m.

Kenton and I made our journey home to Illinois Friday and Saturday. It was a GOOD trip. So many warm, wonderful memories made in that quick trip home to the Land of Lincoln. I was so tired at first. Kenton told me to just go to sleep and let him drive. It was kind of cute. He lectured me about, "Mom, you need REM sleep. You gotta rest or you'll wear down like the battery on the cell phone." He was "mothering" ME! "Sleep, Mom." So I did. He was taking care of me in his own way at 80 mph!! We listened to his music; I listened to his voice sing these words

Blue Star In My Window

foreign to me. I am TOTALLY out of it music-wise. I don't mind!!

I started the drive home to Illinois, but I got lost leaving Toledo—took a wrong turn and ended up in Assumption, Ohio, I think. I wasted an hour of time!! I was SO mad at myself for being so bad at directions. Kenton was asleep at the time. He woke up and said," Mom, let me drive. Don't call yourself Stupid." He handed me his hackey-sack and said, "Good to go." My boy—what a good man!

We got home in time for my dear brother-in-law Bob's retirement party from Caterpillar Tractor Company in Peoria. A wonderful time to see my sister Shirley and Gene, Eric, Sydney (due in 10 weeks), Kris, Larry and Velta, Charlie and Nancy. It was nice talking to them all. One of Bob's co-workers, a tiny and trim fit man came over and introduced himself to Kenton. A Marine for 40 years. He and Kenton talked. The Marine said he was 5'2" and 110 lbs. when he was in the Corps. He gave Kenton the advice, "Keep your a.. down!" and shook his hand. A tattoo on this old Marine's arm also; Kenton said it was a devil with a pitchfork. These Marines and their tattoos!

We then went to Gene and Shirley's new home "On Golden Pond," I call it! It's a beautiful setting. I'm so happy for them. I would never leave a place so pretty! Took pictures and we talked. Shirley was knitting a "skull cap" pattern for the troops to fit under their helmets ("covers"). She said her first one will be for Kenton.

Blue Star In My Window

I hope Shirley's eyes heal. I pray for her eyes, Lord. She is a willing, working vessel for You, Lord. I pray You will heal her eyes. It was so good to hear them happily working in their church. I always have admired their marriage and friendship in love that has always been evident to me.

We all went to my nephew's Cary and Lori's for Saturday morning brunch. A GREAT time!!! The house was full of family, a TV-loving dog, my niece Allie on her "Wizard of Oz" DVD singing "somewhere over the rainbow" brought tears to my eyes. My other nephew Terry's family came in also—a good, God-loving family with beautiful children. As Terry left, he told his cousin Kenton, "I'll light a candle for you at church." We'll take all the prayers we can get!!

My nephew Cary has found his love in Lori. Cary (now is his early 40s) is now with Lori and she's warm, hospitable, open, and kind. A good match for Cary and fits very nicely in the family with her two children.

The kids all piled on Cary's big soft couch, and I took pictures to remember our time spent there this sunny Saturday morning. It was a GREAT time talking, doing dishes, laughing. I miss my Illinois family—so dear to me. Kenton is well loved there. He is so taken by beautiful little Olivia—my niece Brandi's 3-year old daughter. Blond curls in her little pink tennis shoes: a heart melter for sure. Kenton puts a lizard on her face; then his. She loves his attention. So cute and cuddly, this little O-girl. He wants to take her home with us! He'll be a great Dad some day. He loves kids and it's so evident. A teacher or police officer. He'd do well in either occupation, but a great Dad I know he'll be someday!

As we leave, a big hug from my sister, Mickey, who loves Kenton so. She had tears in her eyes as she said goodbye; and she said Brad (her Army grandson who's been to Afghanistan and Iraq with the 101st Airborne Division from Ft. Campbell, KY) never looks back either when he says goodbye.

The drive home went fast! I scold Kenton to slow down, but he likes the speed and says he's in control. We left at 2:00 p.m. and are home by 7:15 p.m. I've never been home that fast before!

We had a good talk about necessary things. He said two things he doesn't want to happen: (1) to be paralyzed and (2) to lose his mind. He has no qualms about losing an arm/leg. But didn't want those other two things to happen. "You let me go, Mom! I'm not afraid. Dress me in my dress blues, play Taps, have the Marines carry me out. When Jesus returns, I'll pop out of the ground in my dress blues, good to go!" What a conversation to have with your 21-year-old son! No regrets on his part on his Marine service. He loves his Corps.

We stopped at a rest area on the toll road in Indiana. A man in his 50s approached Kenton, shook his hand, and introduced himself. "170 pounds ago I looked like you, Marine." They talked and as they parted, same advice, "Keep your head and a.. down." These Marines recognize each other with such respect and mutual admiration. They truly are unique! It was a comforting thing to me to be in my son's presence.

Roberta deBoer had told Kenton he needed to be honest with me. He told me he drank socially... whiskey, vodka, beer. It scares me, and he knows that. He said it is not a habit—never does it two days in a row. Just gets a "buzz" from it. It makes everything funny, he says. It makes you forget, maybe, that you've got to go kill someone in 30 days. I can't imagine that pressure so I say nothing but that I don't want it to be a habit—a coping tool. He assures me it's not, but I'm still much concerned by it. One of my co-workers was right. He told me, "Cathy, you're naïve if you don't think he drinks from time to time."

We return home fully charged. Kenton immediately takes off to see Doug and Jimmy, his two best friends. Jimmy is home from Hilton Head, South Carolina where he works in a seafood restaurant; and Doug is home on summer break from Ohio State University. Text messages from a young woman he's met at Bowling Green State University, and voice mail from an old friend from Garden Park Church of Christ with whom he grew up. This puts Kenton in a whole new arena of manhood which he enjoys!! Women calling him!!

Sunday is my 52nd birthday. Church is where he wears his olive green uniform and he looks so nice and handsome. He enjoys wearing the Marine uniform. "Welcome home" greets him from a few, as well as "thank you for your service to our country." We go to Don Pablo's for lunch, and a Marine staff sergeant sits behind us (unknown to Kenton!). Kenton was so concerned that he be totally correct in uniform in case another Marine sees him. He passes the test from the staff sergeant! Kenton gave me beautiful pale pink roses for my birthday...third year in a row for this. It's now my birthday tradition, I expect! He's Kurt's boy, for sure!! Kurt ALWAYS loved to give me roses...on Kenton's first birthday ("thank you for one wonderful year"), purple roses ("because they're the most fragrant, he said), and yellow, peach (because he knew I loved those colors). Yes, he's definitely Kurt's boy!!

August 31, 2005   5:00 p.m.

A week from today we'll be on the road to Detroit Metro Airport. The clock is rolling. It is time that is passing ever so quickly. And I can't do a thing to slow it down. My mental checklists are rolling, and there is still so much to do. I check off what we've accomplished and still others yet to be done.

1. Be sure he sees:
    a. Family in Illinois   Y
    b. Paula and Frank   N
    c. Leo and Ruby   N
    d. Church time   Y
    e. Prayed for—good to go   N
    f. Nice dinner   N
    g. Go through his boxes of stuff   N
    h. Roberta deBoer article   Y
    i. Highland—Katelyn's class   N

    j.   Laundry done   Y
2. Make the most of family time we
    have with him   Y
3. Have heart-to-heart talk   Y
4. Love him with all our hearts   Y
5. Give him time with Doug, Jimmy,
    Erica, and Jamie   Y

Labor Day weekend is coming. The summer is drawing to a close. I sense the change of seasons. The tips of trees have hints of color. School is back in session. The bees are out with the sweetened smell of apples in the air. Darkness comes sooner in the evening.

August 31, 2005   9:45 p.m.

The hurricane Katrina has been devastating. I'm so restless tonight after seeing this coverage on the TV. What a horrible disaster, and it sounds like it will be months/years before things get back to normal in that area. It has a 9/11 feel to it. OVERWHELMING. I read Matthew 24 tonight. Is this a part of the birth pangs?

Roberta deBoer just called. She's almost done transcribing her tapes and thinks she'll start writing Thursday. We finally discussed what has been left unsaid between us. She started by saying, "I'm sure you're aware that in my writings you and I are on opposite sides." I agreed stating I knew we came at this at different slants. However, I felt like her writing was honest, and I could trust her with my story. I pray so.

She said it gave her HOPE. The a.m. radio shows turn her off, and she's surprised she can work with someone whose views are so opposing. I told her I'm trusting and certainly know there's more than one way to look at things—she agreed laughingly, "at least nine ways of looking at things."

I hope, God, this doesn't make me too "wishy-washy." I KNOW what I believe; however, I believe that a respect and love for another fellow man/woman bridges the gap of misunderstanding. I know it's been good for me to talk. I believe God has opened this door for His purpose. I pray it helps someone somewhere.

Yes, there is HOPE—always HOPE. It never disappoints us.

September 1, 2005   3:00 a.m.

It's now September. September ushers in autumn. It's the month—since I've known he was leaving—I've dreaded most. I wonder why those hard-nosed Marines let their boys go home for such a long period before they deploy? Wouldn't it be better for them just to plop them in their airplane seats and send them off? After all, we "Mothers of America" have ruined the Corps!! No, they let our babies return to us. To watch our boys/men with loving glances as only a Mom can.

I remember in the summer of 1971 it was about a week or so before I left for Lincoln Christian College.

I was sitting at the kitchen table doing who knows what late one afternoon. My Mom was in her living room. I turned my head and caught her watching me. She looked away embarrassed. I asked her what she was doing. She said, with a catch in her voice, "Oh, nothing. I was just watching you." Tender moment before I too left her world for mine.

We watch him take his first tentative steps away from us as a toddler. Then we put him on a school bus with a backpack and step back to wave goodbye that first day of kindergarten. We watch him with the black cap and gown shuffle through the packed Masonic Auditorium to the strains of "Pomp and Circumstance." And now I arrive at September. I drive him to an airport and watch him go through Security. And he goes from the security of our home and my world to a land half way across the globe and his world.

I miss my Mom. I would hug her now. I'd say, "Mom, I understand now."

It is now time for Kenton to step forward.

Joshua 1:8-9 Do not let this Book of the Law depart from your mouth; meditate on it day and night, so that you may be careful to do everything written in it. Then you will be prosperous and successful. Have I not commanded you? Be strong and courageous. Do not be terrified; do not be discouraged, for the Lord will be with you wherever you go.

Proverbs 21:3 To do what is right and just is more acceptable to the Lord than sacrifice.

Micah 6:8 What doth the Lord require of thee?
    To act justly and
        To love mercy and
            To walk humbly with Thy God.

Jesus in Matthew 23:23 You have neglected the more important matters of the law —
    Justice
        Mercy
            Faithfulness
                JUSTICE

September 2, 2005   6:15 p.m.

Kenton and I went and saw "March of the Penguins" yesterday at Levis Commons Square. Then today to Ruby Tuesday's for lunch and my son paid for ME. That was nice. Kenton and I get in our own zone sometimes, and I'm sure Lenny feels left out. But I do savor the time alone with Kenton.

On the way into the theatre, Kenton confided he sometimes gets "tired" of life. It's a large burden he bares. He did say he'd never do anything crazy, but he does get "tired of life." At 21??!

September 6, 2005

We had a good Sunday/Labor Day weekend. After a crazy, mad-cap dash to church, Pastor Scott anointed Kenton's forehead with oil and prayed with the elders for his safety in Iraq. It was a beautiful, comforting prayer.

> "Angels surround him. Give Kenton protection and shelter. Reveal plans of the enemy. Blood of Jesus, protect Kenton and guide him to be a light to the Iraqi people."

Pastor Scott prayed for me as well, and a phrase was special to me: "Be with her in the midnight hour." How did Pastor know my difficulty sleeping? God knows though. The congregation applauded Kenton and his willingness to serve. I could see the pride in my son's eyes.

We had a lovely lunch with family and friends. Beef and ham sandwiches, cold salads, desserts, and lots of laughter and hugs. We all watched Kenton's graduation video from Parris Island with Erica and Jamie, Doug and Rachel, and his new female friend. I read his commanding officer's letter to us, and the group was somber but cheered at the end. We're all so proud of Kenton and love him so.

Monday, Labor Day, was the day when it kind of unraveled. It's always difficult a day or so before he finally leaves. Nervous energy, grasps at conversations, wistful looks. I took pictures of Kenton and Joey in the backyard, and we laughed. Watched "Spiderman 2" and then "Rambo" started. Kenton became Marine and showed us some of his "moves." Laughter, but it makes me nervous to know how they enter rooms, fan out, protect their bodies behind walls, etc. The enemy is out there looking for their target just as the Marines are trained for the enemy. I've told him before: I think about another mother in the Middle East worrying about her son who is training to kill mine...all the while, mine trains to kill her son. A bad picture.

Monday afternoon we all go to see "Madagascar." Cute movie, but Kenton discovers he's lost my keys and his wallet at Bowling Green State University. Then on the way home from the movie, an Ohio state trooper pulls me over for doing 46 in a 35 mph zone. I had no idea; my hands were shaking SO badly! The female trooper gives me a warning and tells Kenton to be safe in Iraq. God IS watching out for us, we all agree! Kenton and I discuss my finding cigarettes in his bag while looking for his wallet. He gets down on his knees and says, "Mom, you've got to be strong for me. I'm scared—very scared. This relaxes me. I won't be doing it when I get back from Iraq. You've got to realize I'm not perfect, and I make mistakes." I remind Kenton he always hated tobacco companies and he can do better. I tell him I "caught" his first Dad Kurt smoking while doing his laundry, and I wouldn't kiss him anymore. He smiles and says the new lady friend doesn't like it either.

We pray God helps us find the keys. GOD IS SO FAITHFUL! After going down to Bowling Green on Monday night and retracing his steps, he calls Campus Police on Lenny's suggestion and FIND THE KEYS!! The keys were turned in. Thank You, God! Kenton says it reminds him God loves him personally.

A nice luncheon surprise at Ralphie's with my son, a kiss on the cheek from him too, dinner at Outback, and the last night draws to a close. I gather up Kenton's clothes from the dryer, and I head to bed. I hope no tears tonight as last night. At dinner he says he has had a great leave accomplishing all he wanted. Very pleasant time indeed. We read the letters from Mrs. Gust's 5th grade class, his sister's classmates. Adorable letters bring smiles and tears. How special Katelyn's class is! She's got a great teacher this year!!

> PFC DIAL
> WE'RE PROUD OF YOU!
> FORMER HIGHLAND STUDENT on Highland's billboard is cool to see coming down Erie Street.

A slim crescent moon rises tonight to end the day.

September 7, 2005   9:35 a.m.

We said goodbye at Detroit Metro this morning at 6:00 a.m. Kenton did turn around once to see if we were still there, slipped on his iPod earphones, and melted into the crowd of travelers at the security check. He should be at Charlotte Airport now before his last leg to Jacksonville, NC and onto Camp Lejeune.

His advice: "Don't do drugs, Mom" in his typical humorous way of lightening up the situation. "I'm coming back, Mom" he reassured several times. Warm hugs, kiss on the lips and cheek and then off and gone! Lenny hugged him "the tightest I've ever hugged," he said. Katelyn and Kenton exchange "I love you" and hugs. Some tears, some relief at this stage one of the goodbye.

In my devotions this a.m. from 19th century author Charles Kingsley: "Thank God every morning you get up—that you have something to do, which must be done whether you like it or not. Being forced to work and forced to do your best will breed in you a hundred virtues, which the idle never know."

Amen to that! It's off to work I go.

September 8, 2005   5:55 p.m.

Further reflections on the Detroit Metro trip Wednesday.

There was another couple saying goodbye to their son. He, a tall, good-looking summer-blond young man. Long hugs to their handsome boy. Mom, wiping away tears, as she said goodbye. Dad, stoic, at her side, yet clearly touched. I'm sure he was off to college; he didn't have the military haircut. I wonder how that Mom is doing today?

We say goodbye in many ways—off to kindergarten, off to college, off to war. Changes in life as the seasons change this September 2005.

September 13, 2005   5:20 a.m.

This is a command that attaches to the vertical: BE STILL. Don't take cues from people or events. What happens when we discipline ourselves to silence? CEASE so you might know I AM GOD.

Psalm 46:10   Be still and know that I am God;
              I will be exalted among the nations,
              I will be exalted in the earth.

The Scottish say, "Some things are better felt than telt." In times of silence, He makes Himself so real.

Psalm 27   The Lord is the stronghold of my life.
I am still confident of this: I will see the goodness of the Lord in the land of the living.
Wait for the Lord; be strong and take heart and wait for the LORD. (I memorized this scripture after Kurt died in 1989 and it's still a comfort to me now these many years later.)

   A very present help…   He is a TODAY
   GOD: Psalm 46:10

DO NOT FEAR; YOU KEEP SILENT.

Silence must be given room; you and I must go into a journey of silence. Proverbs 4:23 "Above all else, guard your heart, for it is the wellspring of life."

All of the above are thoughts after listening to Chuck Swindoll's Insight for Living program. They're like a balm of Gilead to me...

September 15, 2005   5:30 a.m.

Cultivate times of serenity.
"Roots grow deepest when the winds blow hardest."
Oh, God, the hurricanes Katrina and Ophelia dot the summer's end. And Kenton leaves once Ophelia roars out of Camp Lejeune this weekend for Iraq.

Dear God, hold us all close. Be with this son of mine. Go ahead and before and prepare his way. Guard over him; keep him close to your heart. Angels, please Lord, place angels of protection around him and his fellow Marines of the 2/6. Watch and protect our marines, airmen, soldiers, and sailors, please Lord. Protect his mental state and keep him strong spiritually and emotionally. May he be a light in the dark world. Amen

A surprise phone call later this day brings these quick thoughts from Kenton. Since we don't know if/when we'll talk again while he's still in the states, these thoughts are especially precious to us.

—All grunts shave their heads before their first deployment.
—I'll pray, read my Bible, go to chapel. I know where my Anchor is.

—We'll be together again.

—The way you say "thank you" to a marine or soldier is when you just live your life. You go vote, you go to work, and you go to church or the grocery store. You live your life in freedom.

—This is something I feel I have to do to become the man I must become. It's something I feel I have to do to become the man I want to be.

—I will need a little help from above, and I AM coming back to Ohio because this is where my heart is.

—Life is like a bowl of gravy. It's just good.

—We are tired of sitting here and just need to get going.

—We'll have 20 hours to sleep on the plane.

September 17, 2005   8:00 p.m.

Kenton called home from Camp Lejeune. His voice is upbeat, positive, and almost high pitched. He is confident and reassuring in his tone. And he's so humorous! The phone rang, and I didn't want to answer it. But Kenton is so robust in it. He's proud that he's finished his work and feels good about things. He's packed and decides to keep his cell phone on all night to make calls saying he won't be able to sleep. He mentions his beloved Bowling Green buddies. Says his lady friend will spray his letters with perfume, and he's thinking of wiping his stationary under his armpits so we can smell Iraq!! Crazy boy!!

He's bought picture frames—a baseball one for his three girlfriends and includes a note, "I'm a hit with the girls." He talks about Doug; how Doug will never eat the gravy in his TV dinner. So Kenton waits until Doug finishes and then laps the gravy up. "Life is good like gravy," he says. (Ala Forrest Gump... one of his favorite movies!)

He says, "the way you say 'thanks' to a marine or soldier is by just living your life—going to work, going to Kroger's, church, talking on your cell phone, going to vote. That's how you say thanks."

You just have to go on and live your life, Dad and Mom. He says to plant yellow tulips, and Mary Dixon said she will as well. Kenton talks about what a great group of people I work with...not like the guys he does (teasing!). I know I'm blessed in this.

I ask Kenton if I can pray specifically for friends, and he says Marines aren't about the individual—pray for Echo Company, the 2/6. But he does give me special names then of Marines he cares about and says to pray for them.

He says it's all "good trash" and the other notes I scribbled down as we talked. Friday night he was reflective and wanted to be alone. I told him I thought this was probably very normal for someone beginning this journey. He was frustrated and tired of being a "boot."

"They make you do all this trash. Clean your room umpteen times and do stuff that makes no sense." But it's probably keeping these boots busy before their first deployment. When he gets back, he says, he won't be a boot anymore. They'll have someone else to pick on!

So Lenny and I set out the electric candle in the front room window, under the blue star, for our boy. It will burn there until he comes home.

"This is something I have to do to become the man I want to be."

1. Surrender your possessions. Release to the Lord. The Lord is the owner.
2. Release your position. Don't let your ego become like a god. Find your security in Him. God is up to something, and it's not what we're up to. Isaiah 55:6
3. Release your plans.
4. Release your people...parents, children, friends. Hold them loosely.
5. Surrender results in surprises we would never otherwise experience. The greater struggle of surrender, the greater the surprise.

Thoughts from listening to "Insight for Living" with Chuck Swindoll on 9/20/2005.

September 20, 2005   6:30 a.m.

It's 2:30 p.m. in Iraq, and yesterday's **USA Today** said Baghdad was 107 degrees. My son's first full day deployed at his destination. I pray for him this morning, Lord, as I know he goes about his day. I pray that he might feel Your hand, Lord. Guide his footsteps, Father, as he acclimates to this foreign home for the next seven months.

I pray for him that Kenton might not be too bewildered at his new surroundings. Make him keenly aware of Your presence, Lord. Protect these protectors, these Echo and Fox Companies, these marines, soldiers, and innocent of Iraq, Father. Keep those vile people intent on evil from accomplishing their despised intent. I pray these evil doers may turn from their wicked ways and tire of their struggle.

I pray for PEACE. I pray the longing for peace reign in their hearts as well.

September, 2005

Abba, Father, Dad, Pops, My ol' man

So many names we give to the paternal figure in the family. He's generally the "GO TO GUY" who gets the job done in his own way. Some are silent about their work. They just go and do their job for 35 — maybe 40 — years, accept the gold watch from the company, and quietly fade off into the horizon. Others are laughing, teasing bursts of energy that love to tickle and punch their children playfully, watch their favorite football team on the weekend, mow the lawn, tell a good story, and dutifully provide for their families. Some never get it done right, they feel. They're hounded by past failures, fight insecurity, mess up relationships, perform far under the bar society has raised for them, and secretly hate themselves and their demons.

My own Dad was a quiet man. I had him for eleven years. He was 47 on that September day when he left me. I really never knew him; I wish I had. There's a hole inside me where I miss the him that I never got to know. I wonder how much of him is in me. I know the parts I got from my Mom. I'm "Helen's girl." The bent in my personality is shaded by her hand. My chin, her chin. That upbeat way of looking at the glass half full is also from her. How much comes from SFC Paul Russell Smith? I have his eyes, I've been told. He loved to read his Reader's Digest; I love to read. He was dutiful; I am dutiful. Snatches of memories are all I have of him. A walk to the grocery store in the rain to get a copy of Frankie Avalon's "Venus" for his small daughter. Two small girls sharing sugared coffee with their Dad on the tall stools of Super Value grocery store in Bartonville. A Purple Heart and World War II medallion in a blue box as a reminder of his bravery and shy smile. A story received from an Illinois cousin telling of his courage in battle. Pieces of this and that from my Dad.

Cathy's Dad and Mom (dressed in Army uniform)

My own son's father gone away again when he was five years old. Kurt had a heart's desire to do his fatherly job that was not to be. Another strong man steps into that shadow and fills in some of the void, shaping and molding in his own Lenny-way with this youngster. The youngster grows, strong and resilient, is now restless, and learns to be a father himself someday. And the cycle continues. Abba, Father, Dad, Pops, My Ol' Man.

I'm surrounded by the possessions this young warrior has left behind as he wages his first foreign war. I see his digitized cammies, the movies and music he loved, his one stripe, worn corduroy pants he wore over and over during his Kroger days, his deodorant, and mass of papers in the black plastic USMC carrier.

Where are you tonight, son? You're eight time zones ahead of me, on the other side of the ocean. Oh, God, please keep him safe! I missed his last phone call home at 4:50 p.m. Tuesday, September 19, 2005. I had no idea he had called while I was at work out at the guard shack taking care of business. At that very exact time, Kenton was leaving a message from Kuwait City. Germany was his previous phone call home. My boy, seeing the world! Jarring to me that he's so far gone. I pick up the world map in the conference room and trace his route with my finger. North Carolina, Germany, Kuwait City, Fallujah. No map quest was needed—just Uncle Sam's logistic team to get him in place. At work on my lunch hour I type in "map of Iraq" to see the lay of the land and am "black screened" by work's IT department: ACCESS DENIED...TERRORISM. Tell me about it, IT Team! Tell me something I don't know in my head, feel in my heart! My boy is on the front lines living his dream or nightmare, as the case may be. I pepper my days and nights with prayers for him. I lie awake and wonder: where is he and how is he doing? And this is just Day 2.

My dear friend and co-worker Shirley and I have been talking. We talked long and hard on Wednesday about Kenton and her husband, Paul. She is incredibly caring for my son. Her beautiful eyes fill with tears and her car fills with food gifts to fill a box at work for Kenton. Amazing kindness to my son from Shirley and Paul. They're so generous—these caring friends.

Shirley and I talk of the Silver Rose weekends that dot her life. I look at the photos and am amazed by the lines of bikers and leather-vested Viet Nam vets. "Never again" stencils these leather-necked men. Gray pony-tails, a wheel chair here and there, black and white "POW/MIA" flags on the red, white, and blue proudly flapping in the wind. Too many vets dying now these many years later. The obits are filled with Viet Nam veterans paying these final costs of war. Silence greeted their return. Hated, spit upon, flags burning on a flower power blanket of love during a summer in the 60s. Now vague memories of college and the draft. Kent State, the National Guard on campus, the Brinker twin boys down my Gulf Stream street going off to war and one never returning. VA hospitals, dark memories, unspoken terrors and pains. Lost limbs and loves, burning foliage from Agent Orange, a cigarette's smoke in the night watching the rain…I can't even imagine. I was tucked away safely in my college B-2 dorm room and occasionally saw the black and white images on CBS News in the dorm lounge in 1971.

Now CNN gives me up-to-the-second coverage of the latest terrorist threat 24 hours a day. I can Google my way to Iraq (on my home computer, of course, IT Team!), and see the video clip of the latest IED the monsters have left behind. I read in **USA Today** the mounting deaths (now 1902) caused by these IEDs and see the terrorist's cunning new tool of cowardice.

These veteran father soldiers, sailors, airmen, and marines stand in strength and say, "Never Again." These silently suffering men from Nam now stand to the side—oft times in the shadows—and resolve "Never Again."

They've suffered so, these aging warriors. I can't imagine. Thirty-plus years they've born these burdens and chased their demons.

Misunderstood. Deeply grieving. Silent tears. Inner rages. Horror in their memories. Regrets. Homelessness. Depression. Booze. Drugs.

Shut up. Get over it. Cancer and other untold diseases. Poverty. Hearts of gold. Men, now grandfathers, reach out to this new generation of warriors. "Never Again!" We won't let them be treated like we were.

"Never Again/Never Forget!"

Help me forget.

Contradiction and contrast.

Blue Star In My Window

Shirley and I talk lots. World War II vets—my Dad's "greatest generation." They fought the war of all wars. Noble airmen, soldiers, sailors, Marines. My Dad and his Purple Heart, Oak Leaf Cluster, who came back, got his job at Caterpillar Tractor Company in Peoria, Illinois, and never spoke of those days again. I don't remember one war story. Only an old green wool Army blanket we played with as a tent on hot summer days in our backyard. But my Dad spent time in the Danville, Illinois VA hospital, per my Mom, and had many dark days. My Uncle Bob was the Marine, and my Uncle Eugene was the sailor. This World War II trio in my family fighting in the 1940s. Uncle Bob, still incredibly sharp who can tell a story of "Hollywood Marines" and wears his Marine belt buckle at the family reunion. My Uncle Eugene, now fighting for his memory, with his baseball cap's scrambled eggs on its brim. Proud men with buttoned down memories.

Then there's Gene, my dear brother-in-law. A sailor in the days of Kennedy's Cuban missile crisis. Married in his sailor suit—incredibly Elvis-handsome and so young! Long Beach, California stationed with two baby boys, a wife, and that tattoo from Japan that so intrigued my son. "What's that?" young Kenton asked his Uncle Gene once. "A mistake," Gene replied wryly. Yet Kenton couldn't wait to show the Kickapoo Creek champ his own USMC tattoo our last trip home to Illinois. Gene, listening to Kenton's boot camp stories, while rocking in his chair. Still teasing this son of mine—his nephew—and enjoying retirement and his life on Lake Camelot—as it should be. Another kind of vet who dutifully drove a truck for 40 years and now plans to fish and volunteers at church with my sister Shirley.

And there's sweet Phil who drives the black car with the black "POW/MIA" sticker. "Powmia? What's that?" Kenton asked when he was MUCH younger. He was corrected and instructed "POW/MIA." He didn't know. Phil, who loves his dogs the boxers or any animal with such kindness, Phil who was in Viet Nam in the Air Force. The AT&T worker who did his time. He loves the railroad and his family, lives alone with his Tigger and E'Ore boxers, and watches out for his parents. Kind-hearted—do-anything-in-the-world-for-you kind of guy.

There's Shirley's Paul. A Viet Nam Marine. The youngest son of a soldier family. When Paul came home and told his mother he had enlisted with the Marines, his Mom went in her bedroom and cried... not coming out of her bedroom for quite a while after that. Paul, who hugs me tightly after he gave me Marines bumper stickers and a yellow-ribbon Marine pin, and says, "Semper Fi, Mom" to me with tears in his eyes. He walks away quickly. Here and gone.

Don, who tells me of his praying Mom, one morning after church service. "I never saw much action," he says. "My Mom was praying. If I was on the East side, 'it' seemed to happen on the West side. If I was on the West side, 'it' seemed to happen on the East side." He reminds me, this will change him. He won't come back to you the same. "There are things I saw, I won't speak of," Don tells me in the church hallway. In a fatherly way, he tries to convey the changes that will be forthcoming. I can't imagine or fathom now the changes we'll see next spring.

Bill, my new father-in-law (once "friend-in-law") listens and vividly recalls his boot camp days. He identifies with his new grandson as they talk of the times of service and remembers the sting of the gas chamber. Memories of the young man he was ("we did this...) and the training which led him into a lifetime vocation of a fire fighter.

I suppose these memories are strong as each warring generation of men has watched from the sidelines when the next generation picked up its instruments of war and marches off. Fathers watching sons, grandfathers watching grandsons, now some Moms watching daughters as they go to their own battlefields. From time's beginning "a time to be born and a time to die, a time to kill and a time to heal, a time to tear down and a time to build...a time for war and a time for peace" from Solomon's Ecclesiastes 3. A silent heartbreak as the young warrior trains his fingers for battle and his hands for war from Psalm 144. Post traumatic stress disorder and depression was probably prevalent in the Civil War as it was in the wars of recent memory. Abraham Lincoln, his brooding heartbreak over this divided nation, probably suffered from it. Some men not returning; some men wondering why they came back with stinging memories and hoping for their children "Never Again."

"Where are you going, my little one, little one?
Where are you going, my little one, today?

> Turn around
>   And you're one.
> Turn around
>   And you're four.
> Turn around
>   And you're a young man going off to war."

I used to sing that song to Kenton when he was very young. I truly don't know why. But I did. Kenton once asked, "Why did you sing that, Mom?" I don't know why but the tune is still in my head. Did I program him from that song? Oh, God, I pray not! I sang him other lullabies as well. His favorite was "Mary Had A Boy Child," an African American spiritual I'd heard long ago at college. Soft, mother songs.

> Psalms from David's harp.
> When Johnny Comes Marching Home
> Battle Hymn of the Republic
> Boogie Woogie Bugle Boy From Company B
> War? What Is It Good For? Absolutely Nothing!

Generations of red coats, blue and gray coats on the backs of these men. Watching out from one sign post of time to another. Now black leather jackets with studs of silver that cry out "Never forget/Never again."

These Abba/Fathers from a 30-year old war reaching out to this new generation of young men and women. Painful memories resurface. Band aids ripped off reveal deep wounds never fully healed. But just like any good father would do, they put on a new clean band aid, kiss the boo boo, wipe the tears, and send them off to the dirty hill to play their war games again. And the Abba/Father sees his own faded scar, rubs his rough hand over it and sighs deeply. Never again. We won't let this generation return how we returned. WE won't allow them to suffer for 30 years in silence as the demons taunt us. We WILL learn our lesson and get them the help they'll need. We will send care packages, get them help for their post traumatic stress disorder, find them jobs, put a yellow ribbon on our car, and pray to God they won't hurt like we did. Because we're Abba/Fathers.

The Ancient of Days Abba/Father looks down on us, sees our pain, knows our weakness, all too aware that we'll break our toys and boys as almost each generation has.

*"There is a time for everything and a season for every activity under heaven: a time to be born and a time to die, a time to plant and a time to uproot, a time to kill and a time to heal, a time to tear down and a time to build, a time to weep and a time to laugh, a time to mourn and a time to dance, a time to scatter stones and a time to gather them, a time to embrace and a time to refrain, a time to search and a time to give up, a time to keep and a time to throw away, a time to tear and a time to mend, a time to be silent and a time to speak, a time to love and a time to hate, a time for war and a time for peace."
Ecclesiastes 3:1-8*

Help us, ABBA FATHER, to learn our lessons from the shadows of times past.

October 22, 2005

OUT OF IRAQ NOW
BRING THE TROOPS HOME

scrawled across the I475 Westbound cement overpass in bold spray paint of yellow on this gray, overcast Friday afternoon (10/21). This hits me in the pit of my stomach. I feel something seething inside of me. This is YOUR stance; this is MY LIFE!

Do you know, Anonymous Artist, how this makes the mother/sister/father of one of those troops feel?! You secretly scrawled your opinion across this cement barricade in a safe environment (other than the Toledo Police Department catching you). My son is surrounded by cement barricades, booby traps, debris, lack of sleep, and all kinds of things of which you and I have never dreamed! But he's there (along with thousands of other brave men and women like him) protecting your rights to that opinion.

How about: THANKS to the troops in Iraq?! HUH?!!! You ever thanked a person in the military? Have you ever done something nice for a child whose Dad or Mom is serving over there? You big chicken!!! Have you ever written a letter or sent a phone card to some guy in the desert sands of Iraq or mountains of Afghanistan?! Something makes me very angry when I see this. I know it's his/her right to freedom of speech; however, it seems cowardly to me.

A letter from a wife of a deployed service member, Deborah Reed, from Austin in **USA Today** on 10/17/05 affects me deeply. The part of the story never told…war is hell on earth. It's sad and separating. It's cold and conniving. It's hard.

We went into Kroger's on Saturday. They had taken Kenton's Parris Island graduation picture and framed it beautifully with a big yellow ribbon on it. We were so touched. It seems like a coldness of some people is then balanced by the kindness of other people. I'm going up the olive aisle, and I look up and can see my son's picture at the front service desk of Kroger's.

Gulp back that hard lump in the throat and go on.

October 24, 2005

Kenton made his Monday call today. It was good to again hear his voice.

Early at work this morning, Jeanneen Brown told me our United Way representative, Vanessa, wanted to talk to me. Vanessa had read **The Blade** story and knew I worked at Kraft. Her daughter, on her second tour in Iraq, had sent a tough email today detailing her fatigue and loneliness at her difficult job. She's an officer and allowed very little sleep or time to eat—plus doing a very difficult job. Her email had moved her Mom to tears and worry. I just hugged Vanessa. I've only met her once before, but I feel a kinship. Her daughter—my son—we'll exchange "Mom talk"—worries, concerns, little things that mean a lot.

Vanessa mentioned her daughter wanted "girly things" sent to her. God bless this young woman, Lord. White lights for Christmas to run by a generator. Christmas music on a CD and headphones made it feel a little better two years ago, she said.

I told Vanessa what Kenton said USMC meant: "You Suckers Miss Christmas"; and she laughed. She wiped the tears away and off we go again.

I'll pray for her daughter, Lord.

October 25, 2005

> Lenny's 49th birthday today.
> I took ½ day of vacation. I need a rest.
> GI #2000 died today. It's too many.
> As Bill and Mom said, its time to train them and get our troops out.

November 4, 2005

A welcome phone call from Iraq tonight on the cell phone as I drove home. We had a very pleasant conversation indeed. Lots of stories at his 1:00 a.m. phone center (my 6:00 p.m.).

Kenton told me of a 7-year old Iraqi boy who'd asked for money. Kenton gave him a torn $5 bill, and the kid didn't want it due to its being ripped. Kenton said, "It's okay—just tape it." Then the boy pointed to his 2 ink pens tucked in his cammie vest which

Kenton also gave him. When the boy pointed to his grenade in his vest, Kenton told him to "get outta here!"

He also told of guarding his post when he was asked to let in a unit by their number. The Marine said, "I don't have one you ??##!!." It turned out to be his Echo Company leader who then shook his hand. He couldn't believe his leader shook his hand. The unit went by and flashed their high powered flashlights on their rifles at Kenton as they passed by in the darkness to say hello. He said that was cool! He doesn't need anymore baby wipes, just disposable razors and toiletries. Said he and a female friend are still writing and she's "nice." Glad they talked and she backed off a bit.

He wants Kroger's phone number. And he was thrilled to hear his cousin Lauren got a job at his beloved Monroe Street Kroger's—made his day!

November 6, 2005

This is not a good night. I feel really edgy, mean-spirited tonight. I could bite off heads in a single bite! Lenny retired to bed early.

Katelyn—poor, dear Katelyn—is left with a grouchy Mom. She has no problem with telling me I am no fun. Dad is fun. I am no fun! I bite back that I'm doing the best I can. I have to work, I have to do the laundry, I need to do this and that because if I don't ... no one else will do it.

I feel angry and mean tonight. Weather—high winds—tore down trees today. I could do the same. I want to start screaming tonight and howl and scream and not stop. I feel overwhelmed and tired, yet I don't sleep well. I eat and feel my butt growing larger. My headache—the first in a long time—bothered me this morning. This is a lot of venom for me. I feel stupid, poor, fat, angry, and tired. Now that I've vomited out this venom, maybe I can sleep.

November 8, 2005

Election Day 2005.
It hit me today that my son is such a hero. He's in Iraq so I can taste the freedom of elections.
I must and DO vote.
For my son and to honor his service.

November 9, 2005

Tonight, the women's Bible study at my church Cathedral of Praise was a study of Beth Moore's "The Patriarchs." It was awe-inspiring and life changing. I never expected it today, for sure.

Jacob—what is your name? LIAR.
Cathy—what is your name? SHAME; LIAR

I felt the Holy Spirit rest on my arms, my shoulders. A deep, tingling sensation on that area. Tears come as a surprise. Thank You, Lifter of my head.
"Lifter Of My Head" appears in several stories given me by the Lord—particularly the one He gave

me last Easter evening. Is it about me? I must re-read my story. It's my sister story.

November 17, 2005

> *Psalm 119:173*
> *Give me your helping hand*
> *Because I have chosen your commands*

The hand of blessing, that covering hand, as the father places his worn, calloused hand on that life of a first-born child. In Old Testament times, the hand of blessing would speak to the next generation's gains and losses, good things to come and curses to avoid. It was such a unique act of a father that when Jacob (the second son) stole Esau's (the first born) blessing, there was nothing Isaac could do to console the loss from Esau. Esau's sorrowful cry of Genesis 27:38, "Do you have only one blessing, Father? Bless me, too, Father." falls flat on the ground for there was nothing Isaac could do for that son.

But through the cross, the Word of God tells us we become sons—firstborn sons of God. (*Hebrews 12:23 You have come to the meeting of God's firstborn children whose names are written in heaven.*) And there is God's hand of blessing on our individual lives now. In David's song in *Psalm 119:173 "Give me your helping hand"*: is this our hand of blessing? Yes, I think so! He calls each individually close to Him. He holds us near and places his nail scarred hand on our life. The blessing, because we have chosen His commands, is spoken over our lives as a first born son/daughter of His. The blessing is then sealed by His Holy Spirit and that guarantee that all the Father's promises of forgiveness, grace, reconciliation, mercy, justice, eternal love—a myriad of God's blessings rushes over our lives. We are not left out of the Blessing as that eternal hand holds our lives in His. There is never an Esau response, "There is nothing left to give you, my son/daughter." For God's helping hand never tires. The flow of blessing is eternal and never runs dry.

> Thank You, Father
> Son
> Holy Spirit

Please give me your helping hand because I have chosen your way.

November 24, 2005   Thanksgiving Day

It's almost officially over. I went and did two aquarobics classes this morning (even a yoga, which I stretched in ways never thought possible for a 52-year-old woman!!). We met Mom and Bill for lunch at 1:00 at HJ Prime Cut. It was nice, food good, nice conversation. Over to Kroger's—Katie (Kenton's first love and ex-girlfriend) even hugged me today. She looked very pretty. Home to go over the "Black Friday" ads, a 20-minute nap, and I wake up lonely for Kenton. I watched news and stories on soldiers getting their Thanksgiving meals. No Marines in pictures today though.

He's missed today. It's Kenton's favorite holiday.

As he told my co-worker and friend, Bob O'Donnell, in a letter, "Food and football and watching the women clean. What could be better??!"

November 26, 2005

They shout "god is great" prior to the billowing smoke rising from the Jordanian hotel where the wedding party members are killed and maimed.

God IS great, but the foulness of the stench that rises from the smoke is that of a god of the lower world.

I don't find Jehovah God in those hollow cries. The father of lies and trickery has deceived these men and a woman into their martyrdom.

This news greets me in the early Saturday morning following "Black Friday," the ceremonial kick off of the holiday frenzy season. My brain is absorbing this grim set of news while the fa la la la la of the world marches on. This gimme season, merchant driven with the trimmings of gift cards and cash register receipts, is settling upon our land. Cyber Monday, where you can shop even at work, kettles and bells at door stops, beautiful music and silly tunes on the radio—it's all here.

Peace on earth in plastic while the deceiver deals his deadly work in the hearts and souls of these terrorists.

My brain tries to absorb. It is too much sometimes.

November 28, 2005   11:25 p.m.

I just finished a call—an unexpected call—from Kenton. I was asleep when I heard his voice. It was a quiet "Hi, Mom" that greeted me. He usually calls in his afternoon—my morning. This time it was his 7:00 a.m. call—which was unusual. And he explained why—now he's been called back to the 2/6 from his camp guard post. Three from the 2/6 went back. He said it would "definitely get interesting" now. He explained he wouldn't be able to call as much and said he'd have to write more. And he said, "I miss you, Mom." and "I love you, Mom." several times. He seemed somber in his speech.

He mentioned he talked to Doug for 20 minutes or so which was good for him. He talked about women... dating and the problems associated with long distance relationships. Give up one and go onto another. I'm not sure if he's trying to convince himself on that front. I told him he was in my prayers and thoughts and he acknowledged that.

Several pauses in our conversations—almost awkward. I don't want to "talk over him" and want to leave him his space to speak instead of blathering on about inconsequential things. I lean into the phone almost to hear him so far away he sounds. I told Kenton about Whiteford Tree Farm and the free REAL Christmas tree, and I feel his smile. "Awesome," he says.

Why didn't I get him a real tree while he was growing up, I think if it meant that much to him?! We always had a fake tree. Now because of his military service, our family gets a free fir. So many things I wish I'd done better as a Mom for him. He never got to play summer softball as a kid because I always worked in wheat harvests during the summer. I was too fat to take him on Cedar Point rides as a kid or bike riding. I hope I didn't fail him too many times, Lord. Katelyn tells me often of her need for me when I'm too often at work. I feel guilty so often because I'm an absent Mom so much. I hope I haven't hurt my kids in my absences. I've tried, Lord, but know I've failed them both at times.

Forgive my inadequacies, Lord. I just love them both so much, God. They're my gifts from you, Father. Like tonight, Lord, I want to pull Kenton close and give him a long hug and tell him it will be all right. But I don't KNOW that. These are only words I can comfort him with. I just have to have the faith he will be all right with this new 2/6 move. He said all the PFCs in Echo might get a promotion soon—-something about the first of December or January. He seemed happy about that and yet grew quiet again. More pauses in conversation. Sometimes those pauses—the quietness—say volumes about fear or uncertainty. I again assure him he'll be protected, and he's in our prayers.

Please take care of him, Lord.
Amen

December 2, 2005

I was just going to check my bank account on my lunch hour at work. I logged onto MSN, and the headline "10 Marines Killed In Fallujah" jolted me. I felt so weak as I read about the 2nd Battalion members. I mumbled something, got up, and felt weak inside. I made it to the bathroom before crying. Shirley Norton (a co-worker Debbie sent her in, bless them Lord) came in the bathroom and talked me down. It was too close for comfort. I reeled inside for an hour or two before returning to "normal" –whatever that is!

Where is my son? Is he okay? What must he be feeling, thinking, doing? I hate WAR! Some ten families are getting the horrible knock on the door. They say they try to reach loved ones within four hours. I know it's not us; but, God, those families who are affected...

I pray Your comfort on them and those poor Marines who bring the dreadful news to these families of the fallen. Oh, I pray these events draw this generation of soldiers and Marines to You, Father.

I saw big, fluffy snowflakes coming home tonight and thought how those ten will never have that joy. I need to appreciate life's simple joys.

Then this evening we went to a close friend's niece's (kindergarten age) visitation...a beautiful blond angel of a girl surrounded by her toys in her casket. Such a sorrowful time for that family. Moans of grief cried out after the rosary finished. I thought of the dryness in the voice of the priest as he did the rosary and then thought of the story of Jairus' daughter. "She's not dead; she's sleeping." This angel of a girl. Too much sadness for one day, Lord. Too much.

December 12, 2005   2:36 a.m.

I've been awake since midnight or so. Just can't sleep tonight. My thoughts are jumpy and jumbled. They run from "Where is he tonight? Is he okay?" to what I'll wear to work, Christmas cards to be done, and what I've learned of all this ruckus.

These things I've learned:

1. Life does go on.
2. The moon still shines and darkens. And I love to watch its phases. Sometimes bright and often dark or partial. I am also that way these days.
3. When life becomes intense like this, I must simply hold on. I am not as powerful as I'd like to be. I am simply me. God is my only power to be beholden to. I have absolutely no clue as to what will happen. I can only continue to breathe and function. Hopefully those around me forgive my failings when I am not as focused as I should be.
4. My love for the Father has deepened. I pray I'm found faithful in this trial. I pray my son is found faithful in his trial.

December 14, 2005   1:35 a.m.

Just got off a delightful phone call from Kenton. Lenny, Katelyn, and I all got to talk to him. He sounded so good, so positive!! He said that now he's in Echo Company again, he does three days post, three days patrol, and three days in city and it cycles like that for 12 days and then he has a day off. Echo goes into the city of Fallujah and also into the homes of the people there. They investigate any suspicious activity. He says he'll have lots of stories to tell us when he gets home.

Just to hear him say the word "HOME"—he says it with such delight—almost like rolling it over his tongue like a fine piece of chocolate!!! He said when Echo is on patrol, lots of kids will come up to them. The kids know two words: "Mr.Mr." and "choc-oh-late." Or "give me money." He said a kid came up to him and showed him a hole in his mouth—like he'd lost a tooth. He also mentioned going by schools, and the kids run to the window and shout "choc-oh-late" or "money" at them. They wave at us.

The Iraqi elections are December 15, 2005; and he said there are billboards about voting in Fallujah. Kenton said voting in Baghdad may be going on when we mentioned the purple fingers held up to verify voting; however, he said no voting had taken place in Fallujah yet.

He then said he can't wait to "smell Ohio air." Echo will go down an alley and step on something; and he said instead of a fly, it will be a hive of flies or a black cloud of insects. He called the air "atrocious." He said they had lost a lot when he mentioned the ten Marines in Fallujah who died. Said bad stuff happens. Lenny asked if he'd been shot at and he said, "Yes, one time." He said it was about 2:45 a.m., and he was by a window. He was just getting off a six-hour post and heard a crack. He put on his OP blazer and night vision goggles. He said they fired off some rounds but they couldn't find the guy. He said they "suck at shooting." IEDs are more dangerous than anything. IEDs are pretty bad."

He mentioned several times how important mail is to him. Said it's a real morale booster. He said when you get back from a tiring day and your feet hurt and shoulders are on fire, it's great to come back to your rack and see a couple of letters on it. He'd received our Christmas package and said, "Can you believe it's almost Christmas?!" He liked the Max Lucado book ("<u>No Wonder They Call Him The Savior</u>") and had read one-half of it. He also liked reading the book of John in the Message Bible we sent. He'd received letters from Grandma and Grandpa Krouse, as well as Uncle Bill and Aunt Diane DePew. He said ANY letter is good because you can re-read it. He said even talking about the weather is okay. No grass in Iraq. He can't wait to sink his feet into Ohio grass! Christmas, he said, would be just "another day — work is all."

He can't wait to come home, and he mentioned his tour is almost one-half over. When he comes home, he wants to buy a car. He mentioned a buddy of his from South Carolina whose beliefs are like his and has "similar tastes in women." The Marine's Dad is a preacher, and Kenton and his buddy are going south on a "wife hunt!!" He said his buddy wasn't too sure about "Yankees" and southern girls were best to his buddy! Mentioned good news when he comes home: 96 hours of free leave and 25 days to come home in May.

I asked if the more senior guys saw him differently now; however, he said "No, I'm still a boot." He said 2/6 Echo Company will be replaced by a Reserve Unit 125th from the Boston/New England area. Mentioned again he'd have "lots of stories." He didn't want to write these stories down—rather keep them in his head when Dad asked if he kept a journal. "Don't want anybody to find what I'd write and take it." Said he'd gotten a letter from Kroger's that day that they had all sent. Sometimes he's able to talk to his friends online. He hoped to be able to get back to the phone center in 12 days or so on Christmas Eve or Christmas Day. Said his team leader goes through boxes, and they all share the stuff sent overseas. NO CANDY!! Requested canned tuna or salmon—good protein sources. Also wanted mixed nuts or healthy granola bars. He runs over there also. He was happy Doug's Mom Mrs. G had sent him an Ohio State sticker which he has by his rack and the Jesus medallion I sent him in his Christmas card.

Mentioned "cradle of civilization" to him, and he laughed and said "No, not this place." Paula and Frank send him religious tracts which he doesn't know what to do with. He leaves them in the center. Kenton wanted two things for us to buy: (1) new Seinfeld season episodes and (2) special Lebowski towel and 4 coaster set at Best Buy. He told us to use gift certificates from Best Buy.

He said he was going to next call Erica, his Bowling Green college friend, and then go for a run.

He was feeling good and motivated. Again stressed the importance of letters from home—they made him happy. Then he was going to rest some. He was happy it was ½ over!! In April, "Kuwait and then HOME!!"

What a wonderful call! I had asked God tonight, "Lord, I need to hear from him." And God graciously gave us a wonderful 40 minute call from our son. At the end, the connection started breaking up and then we lost it totally; but it was marvelous to hear the smiles in his voice and his stories.

Thank You, Heavenly Father, for answering this prayer. Kenton said to keep praying, and I told him, "Don't worry about that! I pray ALL the time for you!" Amen

Now I can sleep.

December 14, 2005   11:20 a.m.

Proverbs 14:30 "A heart at peace gives life to the body..."

(Tell me this Proverbs thing isn't true! A minister once told me to read a chapter from book of Proverbs on the corresponding day of the month. Something from that Proverb would help you on that particular day of the month. Exact example: today the 14th chapter spoke to me on this 14th day of December 2005.)

I have so much ZOOMING energy today since Kenton's call.

I could scale a mountain—almost!

My joy is back.

Let's TACKLE CHRISTMAS!!

December 16, 2005

Christmas is coming, and I've got $30 in my checking account. Next payday is December 23rd. As friend Bob O'Donnell said at work, "that's cutting it pretty close!" Ah, yes…

Lord, my house is cluttered. I've gained weight. I'm grouchy with my husband, don't spend the time I should with my daughter, can't make a decent meal for our family. I'm not sure what good I am sometimes. I need to stop—to be stopped by YOU, and look at Christmas through YOUR EYES.

Help me, Lord, to do that. Help me to stop buying the press of the world—the idea of superficial materialism. I need a Savior; you sent a Son—baby Son—to me, to me, to me. That's enough right there. But then YOU did SO MUCH MORE. Your gifts of grace, forgiveness, joy, compassion, righteousness, respect, love, healing, and grace again all decorate my life. And the gifts of family, friends, a warm roof over my head, a job to go to, physical and mental health, laughter, love, and grace AGAIN are all just icing on my cake.

Thank You, gracious Father, for Your baby Son. I can't imagine what it must have been like for you that Black Passover Friday to hear "Why have You forsaken me?" from Jesus' lips. Knowing what was to come, You still sent your baby Son. Knowing what he must bare, the separation, agony, pain, and suffering and ultimate glory—You sent your Son to this crazy world.

John 3:16 "For God so loved the world that He gave . . ." You give and give and give—eternally give—what grace, let me never forget.

May that all seep into my being this December day.

December 19, 2005   4:35 a.m.

FEAR NOT. These words leap out at me this early a.m. I awaken with the thoughts on my mind of the angel's theme in their message to Mary, Joseph, the shepherds: Fear Not.

Luke 1:30 "But the angel said to her, Do not be afraid, Mary..."
Matthew 1:19,20 "an angel appeared to (Joseph) him in a dream and said, 'Joseph, son of David, do not be afraid..."
Back to *Luke 2:8-10 "But the angel said to them (shepherds) 'Do not be afraid..." I bring you good news of great joy that will be for all people."*
Finally back to Matthew: *"The virgin will be with child and will give birth to a son, and they will call him 'Immanuel,' which means, 'God with us."*
That's why there is NO FEAR. God is with us.

In this time of global terrorism, God speaks still softly and says "FEAR NOT." What's one of the goals of terrorism? Fear. God slaps it in the face with "fear not." HE IS WITH US.

Sovereign God sent His son to show us how to fear not.

December 23, 2005   9:50 p.m.

Well, what an evening that I will probably NEVER forget. I saw the article in the local newspaper "Christmas Eve With The Troops" that read remembering U.S. soldiers in Iraq, candlelight service when it is Christmas Eve day in Iraq. I said to myself, "I want to do that." I even called this week to check on the service. Lenny wasn't thrilled about going out on a Friday night, but he wouldn't let me go downtown by myself. So we went.

At first, everything seemed fine—as comfortable as one can be when you're in unfamiliar circumstances. Lenny mouthed something to me and had a funny look on his face at the beginning of the service. I flipped the bulletin of the order of service from the church, and then read what he pointed out. "This church recognizes the oppression caused through racism, sexism, homophobia, and other forms of prejudice, both within and without the Christian Church. This church seeks to share in the healing of all people affected." We were in a service in a gay church. What do we do? We're the only military family there! It was pure innocence that brought us there. I just thought the service was a lovely thing to do for families of those deployed, as well as maybe we'd meet other military families. So, OK, it wasn't what I was expecting (even a handshake from Mayor-to-be-again Carty Finkbeiner). What did I learn from this?

1. I was too chicken to get up and walk out.
2. Parts of the service seemed rote and parts seemed sincere. Everything was read from the bulletin and was prescribed. Communion was sincere, and I took part in it. Lenny and Katelyn—no. I don't feel guilty about participating because that part was focused on Jesus and His sacrifice.
3. The men seemed to want to minister to us. They seemed to be reaching out. God, what about gay men? I've come to believe this is the false church, and I led us into it.
4. Jesus came for ALL mankind. This includes gay and lesbians. I'm not at all familiar with this, God. Is there purpose in this?
5. What I remember most seemed to be a desiring of acceptance. The warm, lingering clasp of both hands over mine before we left the small sanctuary. The 55-year-old minister who told me of his daughter and buying her a pair of shoes that fit. His kind glance over to me as we sang the Christmas carols. Men who wanted to talk and a few who walked away after hearing we went to Cathedral of Praise. Division? Disgust with us?

Satan has his paws on the Bride of Christ. I know homosexuality is an abomination to You, God. You destroyed Sodom and Gomorrah.

Genesis 18:20,21 Then the Lord said, The outcry against Sodom and Gomorrah is so great and their sin so grievous that I will go down and see if what they have done is as bad as the outcry that has reached me. If not, I will know.
Genesis 19:24 Then the Lord rained down burning sulfur on Sodom and Gomorrah—from the Lord out of the heavens.
Romans 1:24-27 Therefore God gave them over in the sinful desires of their hearts to sexual impurity for the desires of their hearts to sexual impurity for the degrading of their bodies with one another. They exchanged the truth of God for a lie, and they worshipped and served created things rather than the Creator...because of this, God gave them over to shameful lusts. Even their women exchanged natural relations for unnatural ones. In the same way the men also abandoned natural relations with women and were inflamed with lust for one another. Men committed indecent acts with other men, and received in themselves the due penalty in their perversion.

The minister gave me communion, prayed for me, and later talked of the platitudes of Buddha and

Allah and G_D. Some of what he said, I believe, was correct; however, some was very much flavored by the god of this world.

You are HOLY, God. I don't want to sin or offend You in any way. I don't want to look back at the past night, as Lot's wife did, and become a pillar of salt. I want to BE salt and light, living and active, reaching out to a world that needs You and Your Son, Jesus Christ. How do you see these men and women who reached out to You, Holy Father? "Love the sinner; hate the sin." I too have sinned. My heart is warmed to Kurt's theatre friends from the past and these men at this congregation. I felt compassion toward these men who welcomed my family, yet fear. Is there purpose in this? Later thoughts about this night, made me realize it's not mine to judge. God is the judge. I put my hand over my mouth. I am to love—not judge.

###########

Later, at 7:00 a.m. Fallujah time, Kenton called. It was a sweet conversation between mother and son. I tried to awaken Lenny, but he was too tired to "come to." We talked about his packages received from friends, his last few days of work on patrol, and his desire for home and Ohio. He said it will be so good to not have to watch for a wall to take cover, watch constantly the rooftops for enemy activity, and wear his flack jacket all the time. He again mentioned the smell of clean Ohio air. He said before he comes home, he'll go to some classes to prepare him for home again and mentioned they caution them on suicide because some Marines can't understand life goes on while they're gone. He said it's particularly hard on the married Marines. He said he understands "life moves on." He said he knew it must be very tough to be married and in the Marine Corps due to the separations. He teased me several times, and I teased back. Said he would try to get an Iraq flag for Nortons and us. I told him to read Luke 2—a tradition in our family—our way of connecting over eight times zones. Roger that!

We reminisced over last Christmas Eve's call from Parris Island and both agreed so much had happened in one short year. Last 2004 Christmas Eve, he'd just passed his firing test—this 2005 Christmas Eve: a day off in Fallujah. He thought they'd have something good to eat later in the day, and he was going to make a few calls and get some sleep before two foot patrols on Christmas Day 2005. He liked his red snowflake fleece blanket we had sent over. And then he wished us a Merry Christmas, Mom.

Merry Christmas, son.

December 25, 2005   12:15 p.m.

A ten-minute Christmas Day call surprised us—two days in a row! He was somewhat breathy in his quickie call. The 2/6 had a tree, "fricking" treats on a table, a service at 1600—but he hadn't had a chance to get to church services yet. Some coughing—which concerns me — and a promise of no smoking when he comes home.

He talked to Lenny (Hi, Pops!) and then he was off to patrol at 0830. Still, it was good to say "Merry Christmas" to this son so far away.

December 26, 2005

It's the first anniversary of the Tsunami. So many dead in twelve countries around the Indian Ocean. So many victims and such a sad beginning to this harsh world this year.

Kay, our sweet southern neighbor a few doors down the street, stopped by unexpectedly this afternoon. I looked out and her car was parked crookedly in the driveway. She handed me a Christmas card and then explained her only son, Stuart, who is also 21, had married in October. His bride had entered the Coast Guard, and this new bride was stationed in California. She missed her son, Stuart, and began crying when she said, "I think of you so often. They shouldn't let you have just one child." We threw our arms around each other and hugged. My heart goes out to Kay. She was so broken that she couldn't speak and left as suddenly as she had come to my door.

I understand that pain. Yesterday, after Sunday morning Christmas church services, I drove an unusual way home. Katelyn questioned me, "Mom, where are we going?" My sudden mission was to go and see Doug, Kenton's best friend. We drove past the Guttenberg home; but alas, no cars in the driveway. I just wanted to hug Doug — next best boy to Kenton and exchange information. Had Doug and Kenton talked? What's up with Erica and Jamie? Just to touch his Ohio world.

I think of Karen, whose Marine son Cory leaves on Tuesday for return to Lejeune and then Twentynine Palms, and finally Iraq in March (on his birthday, no less!). My heart goes out to this family on this hard day. The day before the warrior leaves is so hard. The restlessness of the young Marine as he peaks in his desire to get on with it, and the family's utter loss at what to do and how to let go. There is a helpless feeling in the pit of the stomach and a silent cry stuck in your throat. There is no way you can stop him, but everything inside you wants all this to just go away and things return to normal. But there is no normal anymore. You have entered into this powerless state of having no say in your son's life. You can only watch helplessly, wash their clothes, ask if they've forgotten anything, drive them wordlessly to the airport, talk, hug, smile, wipe away your tears, hug one last time, and wave...then walk away. Come back home to the emptiness in your home and heart and make yourself go on.

And yet you're proud, SO PROUD! You know he's part of a greater good. You watch the elections in Iraq, know the purple ink-stained fingers of the Iraqi people are possible because of the bravery of our sons and daughters in the military AND those proud, strong, brave Iraqi people. Your son had a part in history, and you feel a linking to these people seeking freedom in the start of their "new" nation that's as old as civilization itself.

January 2, 2006

What is it about the dropping of a ball or the tearing off of a page from the calendar that gives us such hope for the new year? I turn on the TV, and the news seems the same as a few days ago...rains and mudslides in California, grass fires in Texas and Oklahoma, war in Iraq. We always start with such optimism, but life seems to sour as the time marches on for the most part. This is the best life gets—as it appears in the natural. Life in the spiritual supernatural offers renewed hope each day and even each moment. I'm so thankful, Lord, to You for that renewal. I don't know what I'd do without You, Lord. You are the push and go in my life. When I get discouraged, as I do so often, You Lord, offer renewal and strength.

Perry Stone was at Cathedral of Praise last night—the first Sunday night of 2006. It was jam-packed and an incredible service. He preached on God's restitution from Acts 3:19-21 and Daniel 7:13-14.

Acts 3:19-21 Repent, then and turn to God, so that your sins may be wiped out, that times of refreshing may come from the Lord, and that he may send the Christ, who has been appointed for you—even Jesus. He must remain in heaven until the time comes for God to restore everything, as he promised long ago through his holy prophets.

Daniel 7:13-14 In my vision at night I looked, and there before me was one like a son of man, coming with the clouds of heaven. He approached the Ancient of Days and was led into his presence. He was given authority, glory and sovereign power; all peoples, nations, and men of every language worshipped him. His dominion is an everlasting dominion that will not pass away, and his kingdom, is one that will never be destroyed.

The Son of Man (Jesus) and the Ancient of Days (God). The Kingdom will never be destroyed. Thank YOU, God! That's the hope that is inside of me. Fire ignited. The embers were burning low, and His breath—His gentle breath over my life—tends these fires and the coals that had grown cool. The worry, depression, discouragement: God tends to. He helps me to cope. I'm not too proud to say I need God. In every fiber of my being, I need God. "With my life, Lord, be glorified."

I'm cleaning today. Knocking down spider webs behind the now-down Christmas tree, wiping Murphy's wood soap on my windows, Windexing the front window. Even with the rain, the window gleams as I place Kenton's blue star back up and the electric brass candle below it. That light won't go out until Kenton comes home.

I've taken down the Christmas tree with Katelyn's help. Lenny grumbled as he unwound the lights strewn haphazardly throughout the tree, but at least he helped (which I appreciated)!! As Katelyn said, the place looks so bare as we surveyed it tonight. It is cleaner, neater. I've worked all day; it was important to me to clean today. I don't know why. I only need about 60 more days like this, and I'd maybe make a dent in this place!! We haven't heard from Kenton. I'm missing him today. No new year's call, but I know he's working. I dusted off his pictures and almost cried when I read the following plaque I bought when he was six years old.

"I remember when you were My Little Boy. An extension of my very being. My every waking moment belonged to you. One evening when I called you to supper, you came to the table—all grown up. Where did all the in-between go? Suddenly, I was to let you go. Now, I should always call you 'my son' But...in my heart, you will always be "My Little Boy." D. Morgan, author and artist of these beautiful thoughts

Where did all the "in between" go?! It went so fast. That boy who used to fall asleep on my arm in the car on our trips to Illinois became the young man who gave me a hackie sack to hold when HE drove ME to Illinois so I wouldn't be nervous. I used to give him lunch money (though he'd protest we made him pack his lunch more often) and he loved the BUFFETTT (emphasis on the T). Now I borrow $500 from him to get me through December and promise to pay him back by April. He says, "That's okay, Mom." I miss his crazy laugh and sense of humor—his hilarious laughter over Seinfeld on the couch. I miss the front door opening quietly under my bedroom at night and knowing he's safe in our home. Now I don't have a clue about his safety or where he lays his head at night. How I'd love to hear his laugh. I pray he's laughing with his buddies. "Laughter is good medicine." say the Proverbs.

So I'll go back to work tomorrow and Katelyn will go back to school—the holidays neatly tucked away for yet another year. 2006: the year he comes home. We're one-half way through and counting the months down.

January 6, 2006   12:30 p.m.

How do I feel when I read the news of a Marine death in Fallujah? It's like a target that has been pierced in my heart. Everything stops. I freeze. I re-read it to make sure I read it correctly. I want to push away from the computer screen but am drawn to know more, more, more. I go to another website and want to know WHO? I try to find out what division it is. What is Kenton's combat team number? Why haven't I heard from him for 12 days? I know he's on a recycle program. Works 12 days/off. We should hear from him today. Please let him call.

I jumped this morning when the phone rang at 5:50 a.m. My first thought was, "It's Kenton!" It was Lenny just checking on me. I need to hear from him on these days. Lord, to know he's okay. I want to hear his "Hi, Mom!" I want to hear his voice. I'm cold inside. I know some family is receiving the dreaded news. I pray for that comfort for these loved ones…whomever they are. So much sad news in the world: the 12 miners in West Virginia and so many innocent Iraqis paying the high price for the development of freedom in their country. These cries, tears, and blood cry out to You, Father. How do you stand it? I can barely. My time on this earth is so short, and you are the Ancient of Days. Dear God, You are the maker of our hearts. Our hearts are broken, Ancient of Days. I know Yours must also be broken. Over and over, Your heart has been broken. I'm small, weak, and helpless without You.

Please comfort those who have lost loved ones on this day, Lord. Please help those delivering the awful news to these families. Help them to be gentle and gird them up inside as they must be torn apart as well.

Matthew 5:4 Blessed are those who mourn, for they shall be comforted.

January 7, 2006   6:45 a.m.

News again of two Marines killed in Fallujah jumped out at me at work. This time I sincerely tried NOT to go into a tailspin. I can't each time—each sad time—I see this type of news. I have to hold on. Hold your breath that no one comes to my front door. No strange cars on my street waiting for me. I walked past our front door and breathed a "thank You" prayer to God that no one came last night. But again, my heart hurts for those Army and Marine families who did receive that awful news.

Lenny and I watched the national news, and they barely mentioned these deaths. So sad. Some young man's family is devastated, and it doesn't even bare mentioning their sacrifice. I think the world should stop turning; but of course, it doesn't. Life barrels on.

No call—no news. As Kenton said, "No news is good news, Mom." Amen to that today.

###################

Later January 7, 2006   8:50 p.m.

I hope Kenton calls tonight. I just miss him so. I went into his old room, and I picked up his "cover." I didn't know his head was 6 ¾, but that's what both covers say. I finger the eagle, globe, and anchor and kiss the symbol that my son now embraces. Where is he on this globe? What is he doing? Is he safe? Did he know those dear boys who died? The news says so little. Now that we're past the emotional lightning rod of 2000 deaths, they say so little. It's my chore to read about each slain soldier, Marine. I look at the name, their rank, where it happened, their hometown, their age. I so often whisper a prayer for these brave families who have faced what I fear most. I pray Your comfort on these dear families with whom I feel such kinship. Does the military know that they don't just sign up our children? The enlist the families—the Dads and Moms, wives, children—all of us.

I think of the frozen Parris Island families from last January 28, 2005. We huddled together for warmth that frigid Friday morning. One huddled group pressing together to stay warm as we all watched with such pride our young new Marines.

We all became family that day. Now I wonder how the mothers, fathers, families of the fallen are doing? Comfort them, Lord, please.
    And please let him call.
    Thank You.

January 8, 2006   11:55 A.M.

In the night the phone rang about 1:40 a.m. I grabbed the handle and heard Lenny pick up downstairs also. There were strange sounds on the line; and having just awakened, I was sure it was a bad connection to Kenton. Lenny apologized, saying it was a ring back from the computer. I hung up and again the phone rang. "Kenton?" I was hopeful Lenny was wrong; however, again Len said, it was the computer. Hopes dashed, I hung up again. So disappointed. And news again today of three more Marines killed in Fallujah.

Sometimes, like today, it seems painful. The separation and just sheer ignorance of not knowing is incredibly painful. You must push on, I tell myself. It won't be us, I tell myself.

I go out to the garage to get Joey's dog food and see the old, tattered flag that we have yet to dispose of. I touch the flag and see its torn stripes and faded blue stars. The red stripe is pink almost from the sun. The flag is faded and now to be retired. Yet fresh, 20-something, brave young men and women dedicate their strong bodies to its service. And some lose their fight and succumb under its call. Yet they count it worthy of their sacrifice.

I look at the flag in a different way now. It's not just a decoration—or a piece of fabric. It's even more than a symbol. It's flesh and blood of brave fighters over time who've deemed it worthy to die for. Revolutionary War, Civil War, World Wars I and II, Korea, Viet Nam, Somalia, Persian Gulf I, Afghanistan, and now Iraq. Homeless heroes who have given their all to protect all it stands for.

Freedom.

I think of Kenton's phone call from Camp Lejeune days before he left for Iraq. "How do you thank a soldier, a marine? By living your life. By going to church, the grocery store, and work. Just doing what you do." Profound words now to me. Thank you, my son, for your dedication and service.

Thank you, brave brothers and sisters in harm's way, for your service to our country.

January 9, 2006   9:28 a.m.

He called! I was on my way to the funeral service of my best friend's father. I picked up the cell phone in the church's parking lot. "Hey, Mom." I felt my cheek sink into his shoulder.

"You're okay!"

"Listen, Mom. I don't have long. Where have you been? I tried home, Grandma, your work. I couldn't reach you."

WHERE HAVE I BEEN??!! That's the pot calling the kettle gray!! He went on to say phone lines were long today. I told him we'd heard of the five deaths in Fallujah and he said, "I can't really talk about it." He brightened up and said, "I got my promotion. I'm a Lance Corporal!" I congratulated him and told him we were so proud of him. He asked how Christmas and New Years was. I asked if he'd gotten my emails. "Yes." I told him I'd mailed Christmas pictures. "Awesome!" And a quick weather report from Iraq. "It's rained almost all day—I forgot that it was nearly 6:00 p.m. for him. "Gotta go, Mom. I love you." I told him we loved him and prayed for him. Again, "I love you, Mom." Then goodbye and he's gone.

I'm better. Thank you, God, that he's okay. THANK YOU! THANK YOU. THANK YOU…

##

What I did not know at this point, was that on January 7, 2006, Echo Company and their brothers in arms had broken several terrorist cells but at an excruciating price: sniper fire had killed a close comrade: LCpl. Jeriad Jacobs with whom Kenton had spent the last evening. Several of the Echo Marines were playing chess, and Kenton had been checking out Jacobs' tattoos…admiring them and thinking he might want to get one like them. Since Kenton had been on duty 12 days, he was given the day off. However, other Marines continued their mission on these dangerous city streets that January day. On Saturday, January 7, LCpl. Jacobs, PFC Kyle Brown, and Cpl. Brett Lundstrom were killed by a sniper near Fallujah. I learned of these deaths only when Kenton returned in April 2006. I was amazed when I returned to my diary and sought out that restless 24 hour period in my son's life. Though separated by 8000 miles, the power of God prompted me strongly three different times those frigid January days to PRAY. Little did I know at that time what these brave Marines were facing. God's everlasting love sheltered us; and our prayers and heartfelt gratitude go to these families of the brave heroes of 2 Battalion 6th Marines, Echo Company, as well as all our brave heroes in arms.

January 12, 2006   3:45 p.m.

"808" area code came up on my phone display at the close of the work day.

"Kenton?" Sure enough: "Hi, Mom!" But the connection was bad and it faded out. He called back quickly saying phone lines were not so long tonight. (I remember it's almost midnight there.) His voice crackled in and out, and I couldn't make out most of what he was saying. I heard "1/2 way through" and a question about how things were at home. He mentioned writing a young woman he met at the local library twice but no responses back. Women (especially young, PRETTY women) are quite motivating to this young Marine!! The phone rang again, faded out, and he was gone.

Frustrating, yes, but at least I know he was okay and thinking of home.

January 13, 2006   7:30 a.m.

I'm reading Genesis and trying to remember the Beth Moore "Patriarch" Bible study that I attended during the fall months. It was SO awesome!

Today I read of Hagar and Ishmael being sent away. Is this where it all started? *Genesis 21:8-20. "I will make the son of the maid servant into a nation also, because he is your offspring."*

Jews, Muslims, and Christians share Abraham, the father of faith. Isaac and Ishmael—the division began.

Two sons—two nations.

Genesis 21:17: "the angel of God called to Hagar from heaven and said to her, 'What is the matter, Hagar? Do not be afraid. God has heard the boy crying as he lies there. Lift the boy up and take him by the hand for I will make him into a great nation...God was with the boy as he grew up. He lived in the desert and became an archer."

An archer—flight of an arrow—interesting mention of what Ishmael became. Here it is how many thousands of years later: in this day of targets, IEDs, airplane security, and a son in Iraq who became an Infantryman to fight the terror of an arrow.

January 15, 2006

Psalm 44:3   *"It was not by their sword that they won the land,*
> *Nor did their arm bring them victory;*
>> *It was your right hand, your arm*
>>> *And the light of your face, for you loved them."*

January 18, 2006   7:30 p.m.

    Minutes pass into hours and hours slide into days. Sometimes seconds seem days and days seem—just long. This winter season has been long and gray. Clouds have hidden the sun most of January, and blue skies are seldom seen these days in the Great Lake state. I stare at the newspapers. My eyes scan section 1 of USA Today and settle upon U.S. Death Toll. A Lance Corporal of 19 and a Corporal of 20 are on today's page bringing the death total now to 2236 US service members. Jonathan and Justin today. Prayers for their families. Private agony that makes me wonder if anyone even really notices the sacrifice of these brave young men and their grieving loved ones?

    We love to watch our stupid American Idols and Dance with our Stars, give out a who cares how many Golden Globes or Oscars or an Emmy here/an Emmy there or who knows how many DUMB STATUES and plaster some stupid hair style or dress on a full page of in-color celebrity photos on **USA Today**, but can we even devote more than 1 or 2 lines to Jonathan or Justin?!!

People don't even notice a WAR is going on. It's easy to shut out. It's not cute or coy. It's hard, disgusting, sad, horrible, lonesome, and long. There are no easy answers. There are no neat packages here. We can't microwave this one and pop it out of the oven in 30 minutes. In March, it will be three years! God, You know the ending. I don't. I'm tired and miss my son tonight. How hard or tired will this make Kenton? How hard or tired will this make me and Lenny and Katelyn? I don't know tonight. How do families do it for two or three deployments? I can't or don't want to imagine. What of those who have longer goodbyes? I pray for the troops, for the wounded, for the grieving. God, You hear all these prayers. Omniscient God, who knows all and sees all, how do You do it?! Is that a stupid question? I'm sorry, if so, but I have this human brain that just doesn't wrap around all this too well some days.

I need a huge jolt of HOPE. So I pick up my "<u>Bedtime Blessings</u>" book that my favorite Chuck Swindoll writes today and read:

"Whatever form mistreatment takes, it hurts...In the midst of all this, remember: GOD HAS NOT ABANDONED YOU. He has not forgotten you. HE NEVER LEFT. He understands the heartache brought on by the evil He mysteriously permits so He might bring you to a tender, sensitive work with

Him. God is good. Jesus Christ is real—your present circumstances notwithstanding."

Jeremiah 31:9 They will come with weeping; they will pray as I bring them back. I will lead them beside streams of water on a level path where they will not stumble, because I am Israel's father, and Ephraim is my firstborn son.

OK, thank You, God. I've stubbed my toe in this walk today; and it hurts sometimes and is numb other times. But I KNOW You're on the path with me, and it means SO much. What would I do without YOU??! These valleys and shadows are long and dark sometimes. I pray for depth in this walk; and for depth there must be a carving out, a honing process, a chiseling or molding of my life.

January 19, 2006

A midnight call from Kenton. Hard to hear him. Fade in…fade out…

January 20, 2006   3:15 a.m.

Osama Bin Laden reared his head today saying he would like to offer President Bush a truce. Or he says he is prepared to unleash more terrorism to touch U.S. shores. I've been mulling over Ishmael of Genesis 16.

God's angel and its message to Ishmael's mother Hagar in Genesis 16:11-12:

"You are now with child, and you will have a son.

Mary's angel Gabriel in Luke 1:31 and her birth announcement:

"You are highly favored...do not be afraid. You will be with child and give birth to a son."

Hagar: Genesis 16:11 You are now with child and you will have a son.
Mary: Luke 1:31 You are to give him the name Jesus.
Hagar: Genesis 16:11b You shall name him Ishmael.
Mary: Luke 1:32 He will be great and will be called the son of the Most High.
Hagar: Genesis 16:11b He will be a wild donkey of a man; and his hand will be against every one and every one's hand against him.
Mary: The Lord God will give him the throne of his father David, and he will reign over the house of Jacob forever.
Hagar: Genesis 16:12 He will live in hostility toward all his brothers.
Mary His kingdom will never end.
Hagar: Genesis 16:15 You are the God who sees me. I have now seen the One who sees me.
Mary (in her song): Luke 1:46, 47 My soul glorifies the Lord...for he has been mindful of the humble state of his servant. He has helped his servant Israel, remembering to be merciful to Abraham

and his descendants forever, even as he said to our fathers. Luke 1:54, 55

Hagar: Genesis 16:15 So Hagar bore Abram a son... and Abram gave the name Ishmael to the son she had borne.

Hagar told the 86-year-old Abram of the angel's words. Abram knew Hagar had been seen. God had seen Abram's and Sarai's way of dealing with a situation. They had taken matters into their own hands, and Sarai especially seemed to push her husband into the thickening plot of surrogacy. The Egyptian maid servant Hagar was abused in the vilest way as being nothing more than a womb holding cell for the baby Sarai was determined to get. Sarai's laughter had turned sinister. Hagar grew to despise Sarai, and Sarai and Hagar now suffered each in their own way. I'm sure it spilled over to Abram. Two women who despise one another, jealous of what one has or has not, taunting words, tears, and mistreatment. The angel's words to Hagar, "I will increase your descendants that they will be too numerous to count." Genesis 16:10

Go back, Hagar, and submit to Sarai.

I have to give it to Hagar here for obedience and goodness. Maybe this is why so many Arabs are such good people. Thirteen years pass. Ishmael grows to be a teen, and the Lord speaks again to Abram and gives him now the name Abraham.

Genesis 17:5 Sarai becomes Sarah. Genesis 17:15 This time Sarah's laughter is not sinister. Thirteen years of watching your mistake grow into a loved son of your husband maybe softened this "take matters into my own hands" attitude of the once beautiful Sarah. Abraham's wistful thought in Genesis 17:18, "If only Ishmael might live under your blessing." But God will have nothing to do with man's manipulation, and in Genesis 17:19 GOD HIMSELF told Abraham, "Sarah will bear you a son, and you will call him Isaac. I will establish my covenant with him as an everlasting covenant for his descendants after him." And on that VERY DAY Abraham with the new name took his teen son Ishmael and they were all circumcised on that day. One year later, when Ishmael was 14, Sarah who had lied, laughed, and languished, now bore this precious son Isaac to her 100-year-old Abraham. And Isaac's name means "he laughs."

God was gracious to both mothers. One son, born to a slave woman out of man's manipulation, and another son born to a princess from a promise kept. Abram's/Abraham's offspring.

Two boys—a teen and a baby. Trouble was on the horizon.

The teen became a mocking young man with whom Sarah wanted no reminders of her past. Sarah told Abraham, "Get rid of him." And Abraham—as he should have been—was torn and distressed. But GOD HIMSELF again reminded Abraham in Genesis 21:11-20 of his plan for protection for this Ishmael, yet Jehovah stayed firm that Isaac was the son of promise.

"The matter distressed Abraham greatly because it concerned his son. But God said to him, Do not be so distressed about the boy and your maidservant. Listen to whatever Sarah tells you, because it is through Isaac that your offspring will be reckoned. I will make the son of the maidservant into a nation also, because he is your offspring. Early the next morning Abraham took some food and a skin of water and gave them to Hagar. He set them on her shoulders and then sent her off with the boy. She went on her way and wandered in the desert of Beersheba. When the water in the skin was gone, she put the boy under one of the bushes. Then she went off and sat down nearby, about a bowshot away, for she thought, I cannot watch the boy die. And as she sat there nearby, she began to sob. God heard the boy crying, and the angel of God called to Hagar from heaven and said to her, "What is the matter, Hagar? Do not be afraid; God has heard the boy crying as he lies there. Lift the boy up and take him by the hand, for I will make him into a great nation. Then God opened her eyes and she saw a well of water. So she went and filled the skin with water and gave the boy a drink. God was with the boy as he grew up. He lived in the desert and became an archer.

And 5000 years later we deal with descendant Osama, a wild donkey of a man, whose hand is against everyone. And our hands are against him, this man who directed the archery of two planes into Twin Towers on September 11.

Genesis 21:20b He lived in the desert and became an archer...

The Muslims are now a great nation and are Abraham's descendants. Many of them are graceful people, good people who carry the spirit of Hagar's sobbing cry in the desert: GOD HAS SEEN ME.

And by the cradle, there is a 14-year-old son, and he stares at the silver spoon in the mouth of the promised infant.

And the 14-year-old son says, "Dad, when will you be home?"

And the father Abraham says, "You must go away."

And the emotions of jealousy, abuse, abandonment, shifted loyalties, and lost love are powerful to overcome. And the 14-year-old Ishmael goes out and grabs his bow and arrows and stares at a target.

Almost five years since the Twin Towers, and the road signs point us back to Genesis—the beginnings—the origin—of it all.

God, You see us ALL. You love and provide for us ALL. I don't care if you're Jewish, Muslim, Christian, straight, gay, gray, red, blue, purple, black, white, or green. Father God, You don't label like we do. You see our HEARTS and You are the Judge. In your word Genesis 18:25 ("Will not the Judge of all the earth do right?"), You only distinguish between the righteous and the wicked.

WILL NOT THE JUDGE OF ALL THE EARTH DO RIGHT?

Proverbs 20:8 "When a king sits on his throne to judge, he winnows out all evil with his eyes."

That settles it for simple-minded me. YOUR PLAN issued from Abraham—Isaac—Jacob—David—Jesus. YOUR PLAN.

> I live here.
> > I learn here.
> > > I laugh here.
> > > > I cry here.
> > > > > I am only one of millions to pass this way.
> > > > > And then be gone.

It is Your ETERNAL THRONE and Your everlasting promise. Burn that in my heart, Lord. You're the Judge. I'm simply to come before your bench someday. My Jesus will defend me. I'm at your mercy and grace.

Amen

January 22, 2006   7:00 p.m.

Lord, You are his shield. They don't make a piece of body armor for my son that protects like You protect. They don't have a tower that rises to protect like the tower of protection that You provide. This unseen wrapping of protection comes from You, Father. It adds no weight to my Marine. It girds him from the inside out. Your armor of protection wraps around him; and for that protection, I thank You.

Each day, each week we finish without a knock at the door, we gratefully thank You, Lord.

Sword = Word of God.

January 25, 2006

Roberta deBoer and I had lunch today. Interesting discussion for sure and in the midst of it, Kenton called on my cell phone. Kenton and I had a good, uninterrupted talk at Michael's courtyard. He said he'd been busy with not much time off. He sounded tired at 8:00 p.m. Iraq time and back on duty at 0300 which he wasn't excited about. He hadn't much time for Internet lately so he laughed when I told him the librarian's roommate thought his four letters arriving on the same day meant an inmate was writing her! He said, "No shower, no deodorant, no flossing. Mom, for the job I do…you don't need deodorant or a shower…"

It had been cold and a little bit of rain in Iraq. They had a sandstorm last week. He said he was almost 90 percent sure he'd be going back to Iraq in September again. I THINK that's what he said. It's still sinking in, if that's truly what he said. Sometimes I don't know if I don't want to hear or really, truly misunderstood. He said he doesn't believe what he's told anymore. He sounded slightly accusatory toward his beloved Corps today. I can't imagine doing this again; however, I'm here. Easy for me to say. He's there. That's the stuff a leatherneck expects, I suppose. The troops are stretched too far when they go back two or three times each, I'd say.

Roberta and I talked about our differences. She encouraged me to at least try to publish this diary in

Christian publishing. She said I was a good writer. It's unbelievable to me for someone who's a staff writer at our local newspaper to tell me to go for it. We broached the subject of gay people, and I told her I couldn't tear the pages out of my Bible. However I know I should love and not judge as I learned at the church service on Christmas Eve. We talked about the religious right and the liberal left and how instead of throwing arrows and daggers at each other, maybe they just need to have lunch together once in awhile and talk to reach a better understanding of one another. We talked about our mutual love of writing, and I said maybe it's because we want to leave a chunk of ourselves behind for someone to know about when we're gone.

All in all, an interesting lunch hour for sure on Front and Main Streets!

I'm learning to FEEL my feelings. After decades of ignoring and panicking about feeling ANYTHING, stuffing my feelings down and eating my sorrows away, I'm trying to cope with simply feeling the moment. The phone call pricked my bubble. He'll be home soon—1/2 way through—it'll be over soon. And now, not again! Euphoria over a good call. Unsettled feelings start sifting through my mind and emotions about a "90 percent chance."

I'm good at setting my feelings aside to deal with later—in private. Trudge on…

Marine Moms

We came together around a table on that Saturday, January 28, at high noon. We were drawn there, not knowing each other...other than by a few emails. But we really did know each other because we had one thing in common: our Marine sons. And so five Marine Moms came around this table of friendship to talk for two hours about their young warriors.

We met at Dave and Betty's restaurant on Reynolds Road. Dave, so proud of his namesake, made our lunches while Betty, his bubbly wife, served up her special brand of hospitality with warm smiles and stories of young David. Their son, whose permanent station is in Beaufort, South Carolina, has completed his training in avionics and is certified for his work with F18s. Strong and sturdy, this young Dave, to take on such a responsible job at 19, his mother marvels! His uncle, another Marine, who fought in Viet Nam and ultimately...the ravages of Agent Orange, would have been Dave's biggest cheerleader, Betty says wistfully. And Dave and Betty are so proud of their Marine who leaves for Okinawa in January.

Across from Betty sits Barb. Tall, slender, and gracious, Barb comes across as much younger than a mother of a 22-year-old Marine sergeant son. Mark, who recently took his second oath to serve as a Marine, is currently in California undergoing Special Ops training. A former St. John's student, he's already been many places in the world: among them Okinawa, Barbados, and Rhode Island. It was there that Mark charmed his mother by asking her to

Blue Star In My Window

go to the Marine Ball on 10 November, the Marines big birthday party. He didn't have to do that, but what a thrilling experience to be among 250 other Marines finely attired in their dress blues! This Marine son also carrying in his heart and soul the character of the Jesuits so much so that he's been called "Father" at times of worship. A handsome, strong young jarhead with tattoos and a shaved head smiling from the picture. Sitting next to him with the same wide smile: his Mom Barb.

Next to Barb was Teena. She came in shy and quiet at first, but as the stories tumbled out about these sons, she joined in readily. Ben, her Marine, currently serving at the Haditha Dam on the Euphrates River. Ben, a Humvee driver, Teena explains, who writes and calls from Iraq and talks of coming home. "Send socks, Mom," he requests and she smiles. She so wants to be there when Ben arrives stateside in California; but it's tough when you're not sure when his window of arrival will be and you're a single Mom living on a teacher's salary and working at Sautter's part-time. Teena's looking at all the angles to be able to welcome Ben home in April. Ben and his fellow Marines talk of their faith at times in their Humvees so much so that the guy who sits next to him has a special nickname of his faith. Ben talks of the Euphrates River found in Genesis and says, "Mom, it could be so pretty if they'd just keep it clean." A Mom with three sons—one of them this special Marine.

Across the table is Karen whose son Cory's drill instructor gave him the nickname of "Shreck" because the DI couldn't—or wouldn't—pronounce Recruit Cory's last name on Parris Island. Young Cory struggled throughout school with ADD and needed a year after graduation to let the effects of Ritalin leave his body so the recruiter could sign him up. Strong and focused now—no need for that medicine any longer—Cory now trains in the desert at Twentynine Palms awaiting deployment on his 20th birthday in March. He's off to Ramadi, Iraq after a quick year at Parris Island's Camp Geiger School of Infantry on the same Infantry track as my son. This special son, who gave his Mom Karen his Parris Island Bible with a host of Scriptures handwritten inside its cover to remind him of his faith. Karen, already connected with a large support group in the Columbus, Ohio area, smiles as she talks of Cory and his accomplishments. His purchase of a truck with his own earnings from lawn work (now to get his license) and his determination to be a Marine. Sometimes others just don't understand, Karen says; and she reminds these that this son *volunteered* to go fight this war. A different war from the war of our generation in the jungles of Viet Nam.

And then there's me. And my jarhead Kenton and all our stories. The two hours fly by as we exchange photos, Mom tips, and email addresses, and now plan to meet again on the last Saturday of February at high noon at Dave's. Teena said she told Ben about the Mom meeting, and he was afraid it might be too sad for her. But quite the opposite, I think! I felt like each son stood tall behind us. Hands on our shoulders, glancing around in their invisible circle, smiling at us and one another because we're really all one family now around this table of tribute.

Semper Fi, Moms.

Sunday, January 29, 2006　　　　　　　5:30 a.m.

January 30, 2006　　　　　Noon

I am quietly tired today. I don't really want to talk, glad questions are minimal. Three so far have asked how Kenton is this morning. The news of this week-end's serious wounding of ABC's co-anchor Bob Woodruff and his cameraman Doug Vogt by IEDs outside of Taji, Iraq just underscores how really dangerous it is to exist in Iraq. Over 200 IEDs exploded in just ONE WEEK, says the morning news today. Mind boggling to know danger and injury is one footstep away for our military while we're safe in America. The media coverage has fallen way off on their reporting of the war; and now that it's one of their own, it's all front page again.

I pray for healing for ALL injured. The grandmother of one Marine at church came to me yesterday morning at the end of the Sunday morning service. She grasped my hand and said, "Travis has been injured. They're bringing him back to Camp Lejeune." Staggering news for Travis' family, and this is his second injury. How do you help them? What can you do? Pray—I certainly will. But it's such a helpless feeling. Pray-pray-pray for

> safety,
>> protection,
>>> healing,
>>>> speed,
>>>>> wisdom,
>>>>>> guidance,
>>>>>>> God's supernatural power
>>>>>>>> and insight.

Pray that the enemy is doomed and that the insurgents will reap what they sow. Pray that the evil plans they devise will backfire on themselves and innocent lives on both sides will be spared.

Oh, God, help us.

Saturday, February 4, 2006   5:30 p.m.   Super Bowl Eve

Everyone who knows me knows I am a sports ZERO. I know absolutely NOTHING about football. I know your average player starts practicing in August with 2/days, and this activity proceeds throughout the autumn and winter seasons until it reaches its fever pitch on Super Bowl Sunday. I've observed many thousand discussions from the guys at work on Monday morning whereby they go over who did what to whom. None of it has penetrated my brain to make me want to know more. I just don't get it…sorry!

I have a son, however, who did get it. I don't know where he gained his enthusiasm for it. His Dads nor

Blue Star In My Window

I gave him a zip of affection for this pigskin. But from the time he was 6 or so, he was a dye-hard Dolphins fan. We bought him everything aqua that bore the Dolphin logo. Dan Marino was The Man. Kenton extolled his virtues. He did flag football and joined the McCord Junior High Tartan team. He proceeded to become a member of the Northview Wildcats freshman team and made it on the j.v. squad giving it his best. But, alas, it was not to be. Kenton recognized his inferior football talents and left the game to search for big bucks at Kroger's and a car. I don't think he attended another football game at Northview after his exit—was it because Kroger's usually scheduled him on Friday nights or did he just lose interest? I'm not sure.

The USMC bug bit him, and the rest is history.

After a lunch out today at a local restaurant where I observed rabid Steeler fans decked out in their black and gold finery on the way to Detroit's Super Bowl, I started to think about Kenton and his NFL love affair. In a conversation with my lance corporal earlier this week, Kenton mentioned they had a TV in Fallujah and were hoping to get a live satellite feed of the Super Bowl XL on Sunday. He said he hoped he just didn't get to hear the final score but get to actually see it. I hope so too for all the soldiers and marines who are ready for some football. Because that's home. It's one of America's passions.

The young quarterback of the Steelers is Findlay, Ohio native Ben Roethlisberger. A lot of coverage over Big Ben as he's become a media darling. There's Big Ben…and then there's Big Ken.

Ben is the youngest quarterback ever to lead a NFL Super Bowl game.

Ken is a typical 21 year old lance corporal in Fallujah who seeks to lead a regular life when his time in Iraq ends in April.

Ben has a lot of great moves.
Ken is on the move.

Ben wasn't discovered until the end of his junior year in high school by a college coach at Miami: Terry Hoeppner.
Ken wasn't discovered until Parris Island drill sergeants SSgt. Dolby, Williams, and Gamerzrickli of Platoon 3014 molded him into the USMC private he would become.

Ben wears black and gold.
Ken wears desert camo.

Ben carries a football.
Ken carries an M-16.

Ben makes millions a year.
Ken makes maybe $15,000 a year—tax free while he's deployed!

Ben is followed by the media and hailed for his heroics on the field.

Ken is doing his job along with his band of brothers day in-day out during his 210 days in Iraq, accompanied occasionally by a member of the press.

Ben's face covers the sports section of the newspaper.
I scan the newspapers and news shows for Ken's face and see my son's image in the face of each camouflaged man on the screen.

Ben is a man of action.
Ken is a man of action.

Ben worked very hard to get to where he is.
Ken worked very hard to get to where he is.

Ben's work on Super Sunday will be noticed by millions, rehashed on Monday, and mostly forgotten after the bets are paid off.
Ken's work in Iraq is criticized by some, seldom mentioned any longer on the media circuit, and makes a world of difference to Iraqi men, women, and children seeking freedom and democracy.

Big Ben is hoping to bring down the Seahawks in Detroit.
Big Ken is fighting to bring down insurgents in a far-away foreign country.

In what hall of fame do Big Ben and Big Ken deserve to be hailed? Whose work will be most long lasting?

I guess it depends upon your perspective.
I give it to Big Ken. Sorry, Big Ben.

February 5, 2006   6:15 a.m.

The phone rang at 5:00 a.m., and I struggled to come out of a dream. I grabbed the phone, and it was Kenton. Out of a long, tube-sounding pause, it was "MOM!" We were disconnected four times, but we got bits of conversation wedged in this early morning. He even said the phone called HIM once! (We'll see if I get a long distance call to Iraq on my next Verizon phone bill!) Goofy telecommunications for sure!

"Before I lose a connection, Mom, I love you." And these are the bits and pieces of the remaining conversation.

I don't know what's going on.

They don't tell us anything.

Next time I come over, I'm bringing my laptop and DVDs. It's freaking BORING sometimes!

Probably not going to see the Super Bowl. Have a patrol today.

Awesome that Bridgette got my letter to her class. It took about two hours to do, but that was okay. (Cousin Bridgette is a special ed teacher in Pennsylvania, and her class had written Kenton. He responded to her class's questions. That would be cute to see!)

I don't have email access.

Cut-off is March 12 for letters and packages. (Can it be true...we're seeing the beginning of the end...???!)

Send your stuff into a publisher; you have my blessing. It won't embarrass me.

Who's coming down to Lejeune? Grandma and Grandpa? We talked about cousin Lauren and her school.

I should get $1000 a check. I'm buying a CAR! Going to Illinois if I have to go by myself. Yes, Pennsylvania too.

My leader smashed the disposable camera you sent me. I tried to take some pictures on patrol. I don't know if I can bring you any pictures back, Ma.

I love you.

February 7, 2006   9:35 p.m.

I read the news of the 12 Danish cartoons published by Danish Jyllands-Posten of the prophet Mohammed and that were originally published last September 2005 and then republished in European news outlets this past week. It has a very ominous feel to it. In my spirit, I see this as the tip of a spear. A cartoon in blasphemy to those who hold Islam and their Qur'an precious. A push over the edge to extremists in Islam and a high call to arms.

Meanwhile, I think we, in America, are asleep at the wheel. We don't understand the nerve this strikes. It is a dry tinder box ready to catch on fire. One billion Muslims—ten percent of whom are extremists—ready to sacrifice their lives in a blink of an eye. This will not only take my son, it will take all our sons and daughters if the extremists have their way in their struggle for a jihad. We are all to taste this cup unless Jesus returns for us.

Iran wants to wipe Israel off the map. Jehovah God will not allow this as His blood covenant is with Israel. He is Jehovah God of Abraham, Isaac, and Jacob. His covenant reaches down through that red thread of redemption through David, Solomon, Daniel, Peter, Paul, to all believers of the cross of Jesus. There is security in that covenant that no matter what loss occurs here Jehovah God is in control. The madmen of the world may have had their say, the losses may be great, but we can rest in our shield of Jehovah God. For in this land, In God We still do Trust. Not all, but Father God, a remnant hold up Your standard. Your Holy Word warns us of the birth pains. We most certainly are beginning to feel these. Western civilization is being put on notice. And we're asleep at the gate. Only a few guardians notice the signs. Their ears are tuned toward these ominous events.

Tonight I feel our sons and daughters will pay the price. There is no easy exit. I feel—I sense—a long, hard road ahead. Diplomacy, appeals to calm—we may be past that now. The animated existence that we thrive on here in America of celebrity and celluloid stardom now stares down a dark cartoon which has no humor for what they see as blasphemy. This fire of contempt—now aimed at Denmark and Norway—will spread as a wildfire toward all western civilization. We've been put on notice before. 9/11 happened. The next time (or times) I fear will make 9/11 look pale in comparison. Again, we will pay; our children will pay. God help us. His message is hope, but we've been warned by Him in His Word. We've also been shown in that same Word that He will never leave us—no matter how large the shadow looms.

Psalm 23
The Lord is my shepherd, I shall not be in want.
He makes me lie down in green pastures,
He leads me beside quiet waters,
He restores my soul.
He guides me in paths of righteousness
For his name's sake.
Even though I walk
Through the valley of the shadow of death,
I will fear no evil,
For you are with me;
Your rod and your staff,
They comfort me.
You prepare a table before me
In the presence of my enemies.
You anoint my head with oil;
My cup overflows.
Surely goodness and love will follow me
All the days of my life,
And I will dwell in the house of the Lord forever.

February 8, 2006   8:30 p.m.

Kenton called Sunday morning at 5:00 a.m. and then WOW another "808" displayed on my work phone at 2:00 p.m. today. It almost makes me feel like he's stateside—this rare call spaced so soon after the weekend. It's 10:00 p.m. Iraq time, and he says it's windy with rains moving in tonight. Today he reports he got to see bits and pieces of the Super Bowl and knew Pittsburgh had won. He had gotten a package of MREs from Lt. Col. Karen Diefendorf (my college friend who is now an Army chaplain at the Pentagon) and said she, for one, had sent all the right stuff: energy bars, tuna and salmon MREs. They were all delicious, he said. Hard to believe a Lt. Colonel would send this care package to a lowly Marine. He also mentioned pictures of Ashley, Karen's Air Force daughter ("I'm unattached," her mother had written on one picture!)

Kenton said things had been a bit more "mellow" lately there. He couldn't really say much, but they had changed their tactics in January. Kenton wondered aloud, "Why change it up this close to leaving?" He tells me he's on a staff phone—that costs $9/minute to the U.S. tax payer. We talk about $90 worth of my tax dollars, and I feel it's a bargain to feel close to this beloved son and be able to say "love you" and "stay safe." When I drop by H&R Block after work, I feel better about my taxes—for just a bit!!

He's mentioned coming home the third or fourth week of April 2006. Prior to that, they'll go to Kuwait where "it'll be hot as balls!" I tell him he may enjoy it, but he insists they'll all just want to get home stateside. I go to the USMC website and see the 2/7 has returned Sunday to California. They left in July, and it was cool to see all the Dads greeting their new babies and children.

It won't be long now!!

February 12, 2006   Sunday   8:25 a.m.

Kenton called this morning. He asked if I was getting ready to go to church. Sure was. Glad to stop and visit with him though.

He's talking about coming home: 60 more days — window of April 12-16, 2006. He just wants to get his job done and get home, he says.

I felt like there was something he wasn't telling me. Did something happen? I'm not sure. He seemed to have harsh sentiments toward Fallujah. I asked him if something was wrong, "Are you okay? I hear a catch in your voice?" But he's fine, he says, just wants to get home. Kenton gives us the name of a book to read ("No True Glory" by Bing West), and says we'll understand Fallujah more.

Katelyn gets on the phone. He mentions lots of stray dogs after Katelyn tells him a "Joey" story.

He says he doesn't want to go on any vacations with palm trees included.

Nothing to remind him of Iraq.

February 18, 2006   7:30 a.m.

I was brushing my teeth when the phone rang so Katelyn answered it. "Kenton?!" she exclaimed. So I hurried to take the phone while Katelyn scrambled into her bedroom to get on the extension phone. It was a crummy connection, so we all tried to listen hard and say what we could while we could. It would be a quick call, he said, as he had a patrol into the city in 20 minutes. I asked how he liked that and he said it was okay—sometimes fun and sometimes not. They had given comic books ("100% coalition propaganda," he said), soccer balls, and candy to the children. He would try to bring some home so we could see the comic books. All part of winning the hearts of the kids.

He'd been reading lots (Gates book) as it helped pass the time. He mentioned "<u>A Million Little Pieces</u>," which I told him had a lot of lies in it, per Oprah. When I mentioned -1 below zero for tonight's temperature, he said it had been cold in Fallujah also ("It's cold here today.") He wanted to talk about plans when he came home. Kenton asked about going to Illinois and Pennsylvania.

The call began breaking up as we began to talk, and he was gone. A few minutes later..."Mom are you still there?" as he called back a second time. His voice faded in and out, and I couldn't make out what he was saying. However, the dreaded familiar, "Hang up. The call could not be completed successfully..." AGAIN!!

February 21, 2006 3:03 a.m.   later in the morning when I could not sleep

I was reading in **Newsweek** where the word "Islam" is derived from the word "peace."

I see the faces of 20-somethings who are so enraged over the Danish cartoon of the Prophet Mohammad. We're astounded here in America over the cartoon image that is causing destruction and threats of death.

We value freedom of speech and our Constitutional rights to it here in the United States. We're blown away to see what can happen on the world's stage when that freedom infringes on someone's dearly and deeply held belief system. We don't understand the psyche of a Muslim religious extremist. I've been reading bits and pieces to try to gain insight here. I understand somewhat why they hate us and call us infidels. We ARE infidels in many ways.

We are a nation dripping in sin. We are so self-absorbed and surfacy. So much of what is portrayed on the TV and movie screens is absolute vile. Our hands are NOT clean. We argue and draw the sword on ourselves in so many ways. We cheat and expect it to be overlooked. We lie and rationalize that it's not our fault. We've broken every one of the 10 Commandments and have smashed the stone tablets into a "million little pieces" and are unblinkingly unapologetic about it to God, the world, and each other. The terrorists say, "Death to America." We're doing a pretty good job of it to ourselves, I'd say.

God is our ONLY hope; in God we do trust. But our hands are SO dirty. The terrorists want to kill all Jews and Christians. This is the beginning of the jihad they want. They are willing to die for it with no questions asked. We don't get it and are clueless to this danger. I am no deep thinker, but we are on such a collision course. Afghanistan, Iraq, Iran. I turn to the book of Daniel and reach chapter 7. King Darius, who because of his own decree had put Daniel in the lion's den, then hoped Daniel's God would rescue him. I think today there are many millions of good Muslim people who have high regard for what our country stands for. Many have made their homes and businesses here and are people of peace…good, loving people. Many abroad in the Muslim world extend that hospitality to us and hope, as King Darius, that our God will rescue us from the extremists and work toward diplomacy. It's in their and our best national interests.

But then I read chapter 7 of Daniel and his dream. I read Daniel 12 of the End Times (verse 7) of the "times and half a time." In my Bible on Daniel 7 are notes I took when Perry Stone visited our church several years ago. He talked of Daniel's vision and the substance of his dreams as it impacts today.

Daniel 2: "In my vision…" churning up the great sea: the Mediterranean.

Lion: Britain's symbol, wings of an Eagle: America's symbol. Heart of a man: America's compassion.

I remember Perry talking about during this time there would be a restraint of the antichrist. But as Daniel writes on, he became troubled in spirit and he talks of a 4th beast coming from the 3 beasts, and how this 4th beast wages war against the saints and defeats them. Until the Ancient of Days comes and pronounces judgment in favor of the saints (verse 22). Daniel speaks in 8:12 of truth being thrown to the ground. While I know historically the chronology of the major empires in the book of Daniel in his vision:

LION	BABYLONIA
BEAR	MEDO PERSIA
LEOPARD	GREECE
TERRIFYING & FRIGHTENING BEAST	ROME and in AD 70 the fall of Jerusalem

I believe much of Daniel to be prophetic to our times as well. Daniel 12 is powerful and is written to us as believers to give us hope—and wisdom—in these times.

Then I, Daniel, looked, and there before me stood two others, one on this bank of the river and one on the opposite bank. One of them said to the man clothed in linen who was above the waters of the river. How long will it be before these astonishing things are fulfilled? The man clothed in linen, who was above the waters of the river, lifted his

> *right hand and his left hand toward heaven, and I heard him swear by him who lives forever, saying, It will be for a time, times and half a time. When the power of the holy people has been finally broken, all these things will be completed. I heard, but I did not understand. So I asked, My lord, what will be the outcome of all this be? He replied, Go your way Daniel, because the words are closed up and sealed until the time of the end. Many will be purified, made spotless and refined, but the wicked will continue to be wicked. None of the wicked will understand, but those who are wise will understand.*

Daniel 12:5-10

Help us, Holy Spirit, to understand our times.

February 22, 2006   8:00 p.m.

The War on Terror was on the front doorstep today in Toledo. Three were arrested for plotting terrorist jihad activities while driving the very streets of Toledo and moving among us. They're "innocent until proven guilty," but the indictment brought down by the federal government looks pretty ominous. I read it on the internet web site. It talked of their planning practice activities over the 4th of July holiday because gunfire and explosions are normal during that period of time! A student at UT, a used car salesman on Reynolds Road—unbelievable and chilling news. The Arab Americans are on the TV afraid of repercussions to their lives and businesses due to these developments in Toledo, Ohio. It was the Arab American community who turned in these three men. These are good, conscientious, fair-minded people. Concerned about being "guilty by association."

I was thinking about this on the way home. How do you show love and respect (as the Bible tells me) to someone with whom fear and suspicion are also mixed in? Trust is hard to pin down. Once trust has been broken in a relationship, it's hard to re-establish.

> Ishmael and Isaac
>   Jacob and Esau
>   Eyeing each other warily.
>   Can they be brothers again?

February 22, 2006   10:00 p.m.

I was just Cathy for 30 years. Daughter... student...secretary...friend...wife. I had all those affiliations. But when I turned 31, I became MOM. On June 11, 1984, my 31st summer (if my math is correct), this lump of flesh transformed into a Mom. And I've been in the Mom mold ever since.

I'm 52 years old now. It's my favorite "job"—I can't imagine not being "Mom" or "Ma" to my two children. I look at pregnant women and think, "You have no idea what a change you're in for! It's way beyond the "I'll never get my figure back" fixations.

I've loved all the confusing times, the maddening times, the frustrating times—because you know what? They're gone. They passed SO QUICKLY. And all that's left is the warmth of love for my two kids.

I love them so.

They're two unique, gifted individuals with whom I share a bond never to be broken. I am in love with my two kids: Kenton and Katelyn.

Unashamedly, completely.

February 23, 2006   8:00 p.m.

I just saw a CNN story that made me irate! A group of "religious" protestors go to the funeral of fallen soldiers and protest LOUDLY with taunts and signs of "Thank God for Dead Soldiers."

They have crossed the line.

These so-called "religious" protestors who say God is punishing soldiers for America's "support" of homosexuality. Ms. Phelps shouts, "God is your enemy" at a mother who is burying her 23-year old son this day. HOW CRUEL CAN ONE BE??!! And in the name of religion. HOW SAD! Another group, the Patriot Raiders, has come to the aid of these grieving families. They come out and sing patriotic songs over the protesters to muffle their shouts. They have empathy for these families so they have some measure of peace over the hateful words of protest. To tell a mother burying her son that he is buried with the jackals and sent to hell because he defended the U.S. is twisted and mean spirited. AAAGGGHHH!!!!

2286 deaths of U.S. service men and women in Iraq in nearly three years of war. It's so sad to twist religion in this way.

I've heard it said:

> RELIGION is for those who don't want to go to hell.
> FAITH is for those who've been to hell and back.
> These families in their grief have been to hell and back. Grant them true faith for their pain, and forgive us when we twist Your Word in such ways, Lord.

February 24, 2006   6:00 a.m.

You don't send your flesh and blood over to a war zone in Iraq without waking up in the night thinking of your loved one.

You don't get up in the morning without wondering how your son/daughter is faring.

You don't watch the news or read a newspaper article of possible Civil War in Iraq between the Shiite and Sunni people without a sigh and wonder how he's/she's doing in threatening situations.

I PRAY FOR PEACE ALWAYS.

And I pray that calmer heads will prevail; however, there seems to be no calmness left. It's all radical, wild emotions bubbling over in the streets of the cities. What will this day bring for our soldiers and marines in arms?

Small sparks ignite large fires. I walk outside in the pre-dawn light. A slim crescent moon shines brightly in the darkly blue sky. To the upper left is the planet Venus shining brightly. I look at this beautiful illumination God has created in the morning sky and pray for these sons and daughters on the other side of it.

It is the 24th of the month, and I read the 24th chapter of Proverbs for today's insight:

Proverbs 24:6 for waging war you need guidance and for victory, many advisors.

I pray for President George W. Bush and his military and civilian advisors

February 26, 2006   Sunday night at 6:00 p.m.

My college friend, Lt. Col. Karen Diefendorf, called me unexpectedly tonight at 6:00 p.m. How amazing it is to me to instantly hook up with Karen from friendships started 31 years ago at Lincoln Christian College. She had a dream of Lenny and me and her husband Walt and her eating frog legs!! How funny! (Per Lenny, it's so sad about the little wheelchairs stacked up in the corner!)

Karen and I talked of our children. Her middle daughter Ashley soon to graduate from Clemson University and then on to San Antonio and an Air Force commission. She wanted to know about Kenton and his return in April. Karen offered her ear and skills in her chaplaincy duties to us as he readied for this return in April She has been a God-send to me, this friend of 30 plus years.

I told Karen of a disturbing dream I had about Kenton. In it, I only remembered that his left eye had been hurt and his teeth were jagged. She counseled me that I may see physical and emotional changes in him. The dream bothered me. It was so good of her to call…God's timing, I'm sure…just to talk.

February 26, 2006   8:30 p.m.

We had our second Mom's meeting today at Dave's Home Cooked Food restaurant. WOW! We grew this month! So many new Moms showed up— it was fantastic!!

Betty, Teena, Barb, and myself…then the new ones: two sisters whose sons are both Marines. One near Fallujah and the other at Twentynine Palms, California. Ben, Kenton, and this one son soon are to return from Iraq. A new Mom from Columbus whose son is soon to go to Parris Island, South Carolina. She's a single Mom of five children who is trying to encourage her recruit son. Another Mom whose son is in the Delayed Entry Program and in college soon to report to Parris Island. This mother's eyes filled with tears many times as she listened to our stories, and my heart hurt for her. It was a total surprise to her that her son would want to do this and so foreign to her. She was trying to adjust to this news. Two other Moms—one with a Marine and one with a Marine and Air Force son, who pray and invite us to a Monday night prayer cell group in Maumee. Powerful, praying Moms.

We all talked of how this was a GOD-THING and agreed He wanted us to connect. It's such a relief to know there are others out there like us. WE ARE NOT ALONE!!!

Lenny and Paul sat aside at a solitary Dad's table, but it was Ladies' Day at Dave's!!! So much fun and how the time flew! Connection and creativity.

Never underestimate the power of Military Moms!!!

February 27, 2006   9:00 a.m.

"We're on the final countdown when it's March, Mom," Kenton told me in his Monday morning call. "My leave dates are April 21 through May 15, if I want to take 24 days. But I don't know if I want to use all together. On April 21, there's a division wise Memorial service for those lost in Iraq. April 22 I should be able to leave for Ohio. We'll make sure our weapons are spic n' span, the new boots in School of Infantry will put all our stuff away for us and then we can go."

He asked about the "Civil War" in Iraq as seen through CNN's eyes. He said it seems to stay the same in Fallujah, but "CNN's got to hype the events so they can sell the news," per this lance corporal. He was wearing a t-shirt and shorts today as the weather was starting to hit the 80s, and the phone lines were long again today. He said he'd better cut it off. But it was a HOPEFUL Marine calling today looking forward to Spring.

Late Monday night, I went to an amazing prayer meeting with other military parents. What a privilege it was to pray with these mature prayer warriors. I was truly and deeply blessed by the time spent in God's holy presence.

March 3, 2006   7:00 a.m.

This has been an amazing journey—not quite complete. Lord, I wondered how to make the journey, but You have been there every step of my/our way. I feel this so securely in my soul.

You ARE the God who sees; You ARE there for me/us.

Sometimes I've clung to You. Sometimes You've allowed me to take tentative baby steps away. But just as an earthly Father, You're never more than an arm's length away to catch me when I've cried out or done something foolish.

If I had not made this journey, I would not know again of Your fatherly nature. I would not have tasted the tears or flexed my faith muscles.

My roots would not have dug as deep in Your soil.

I would not have met some of the dear friends who honor me with their love and friendship.

I would not have felt the depth of love for my family and pride in my country.

I would not have seen the sacrifice in service or bravery of this young generation of warriors.

Trials—crucibles—the gold and silver rise to the top.

For this I thank You today.

March 5, 2006   9:30 p.m. (Sunday)

Sometimes things happen in a day which author/speaker Beth Moore (one of my favorites) calls God Stops. They are things—ordinary events—which occur that stop you to realize you have been touched by God. Such was one today.

I'm doing laundry on a Sunday afternoon down in my basement. As I pull the damp clothes out, the phone rings and my daughter yells downstairs, "Mom, it's for you." I finish hanging up the damp slacks and retrieve the phone in the next room. At the end of the line was Kit, a Marine Mom. I'd met her only a week before. She and her husband, along with 4 or 5 other military parents, meet for prayer on Monday evenings. I had been privileged to pray with them the past Monday night. Their prayers dug deep into God's soil. Mature, grown-up prayers full of conviction and passionate love for our Heavenly Father and His work on earth. And, of course, earnest prayers for our children in Iraq and the people who call Iraq their homeland. No "baby" prayers, these.

No one-liners or "gimme" prayers. These were heart-felt dialogues with our Creator. Boldly coming into the throne room of the King because His Son Jesus was our Mediator. It was a beautiful time.

Kit called and we started talking about our sons, as mothers do. Her Marine son has been in Iraq only a short time—a couple of weeks. She said yesterday she was at Meijer's and the cashier had the same dark hair as her son. She told herself, "Come on. You can't lose it here." Little things trigger these strong responses in a Mom. I told her I understood. Sometimes I just want to go back to the time when Kenton was a baby and rock him again. Reality is that's not possible any longer. But arms still ache sometimes to feel that child's warmth again.

Kit mentioned the September article in **The Blade**. She had saved it but never read it. The picture of the Mom hugging her son was "too close," I think is how she said it, at the time. She put it aside all those months ago, and for some reason last week, pulled it out again. At the brief introduction time prior to starting prayer last Monday, I said my name and Kenton's name. Kit said, "I saw that article. Your names are familiar." We talked briefly about it and then went into prayer time.

Today, on the phone, she said she'd read it. I told her it was our prayer that God be honored by whatever Roberta deBoer wrote and that this be a vehicle God would use. It connected the dots of our lives together in a way only God can do. I remember as a child that one of my favorite art activities: connect the dots. All those little numbers seemingly randomly placed on the black and white page. My pencil or crayon would jut from one number to another until finally the picture was revealed. Another dot connected this cold Sunday afternoon: one Mom's heart to another. Promises of prayers for Connor and Kenton. Men arriving Iraq; men coming home from Iraq. Choice, brave, strong young men. Flowing in/flowing out. Our best.

More dots to connect. What kind of picture will it be? Faith in our Father for whatever the outcome. Honor and duty. We simply believe.

March 13, 2006   9:00 p.m.

He has lived six months of his 21-year-old life in a country not his own.

He has invested much and he is dedicated to the job the 2/6 has done.

He has signed over four years of his life to the United States Marine Corps. He has voluntarily given up the familiarity of Ohio, his family, and friends.

He now embraces another culture and has a new family—the Corps. His letters indicate a depth he didn't have before.

He is thoughtful in his writing and reaches out to "Ma" and "Pops," but his thoughts and ideas are his own now—no longer spoon fed.

He has questions I never dreamed of asking.

He's seen sights I can't imagine.

He's pushed himself in ways I've never stretched to reach.

I'm going to meet and greet a son in a little over a month—in many ways a son whom I don't know and have never met before.

But when I hug him, I'll know my son.

A war can't wipe that away.

March 14, 2006

I've held my tongue long and hard. I've wanted to say things to a local political activist. But I've withheld that which I feel so deeply inside myself.

I'm the mother of a United States Marine currently deployed in Fallujah, Iraq. I've driven under the overpasses that have the spray painted signs "Troops Home Now" time and time again. I remember the first time I saw one last autumn. My son had just left for Iraq, and it brought tears to my eyes. You see, I want my troop home too. I do. And the guys over there want to come home. But not before their job is done. They shoulder a heavy responsibility to those who have sacrificed life and limb to see the job through and pass on the baton. They train the Iraqi police and Iraqi army national guard daily. They know there is a greater good. Freedom costs.

Every day I wear something on my jacket, a bracelet on my arm, a flag on my lapel to remind me that freedom costs. I pass by your fluorescent sign and know the freedom you have to spray paint your conviction was paid for in blood by some Veteran or current young man or woman serving this great country. It's guaranteed you in the Bill of Rights; however, it's paid for by the sacrifice of those who protect that right every day no matter where they're stationed. That's right...the U.S. military guards that right with their very lives. As someone else said, it's the "home of the free BECAUSE of the brave." They put their lives on the line every single day.

Yes, there have been mistakes made in this mission. Billions of dollars spent and precious, irreplaceable lives have been lost—both on the side of the United States and coalition forces as well as innocent lives lost in Iraq and Afghanistan. An anonymous IED doesn't care who or what it hurts; it makes its bloody statement of terror in this "eye for an eye...tooth for a tooth" world. But there are those who do justice and love mercy enough to lay it on the line each and every day for these freedoms to allow someone else to have a taste of that freedom. To stand up to that terror that now assaults each man, woman, or child citizen of this world.

Maybe things won't change that much in that war-torn portion of the world. In the grand spectrum of things, we have to allow the transition to eventually take place. But I don't believe the job is yet done and the mission is not quite accomplished as we approach the third anniversary of this hard war. I don't know that this war on terror will ever be done. However, there are those who are willing to pay the price that freedom costs. My son's captain has a saying, "To those who fight for it, life has a special flavor that the protected will never know." Yes, bring the troops home in due time; however, to make their mission count and underscore the brave sacrifice of those who gave all, let them do their job. And thank them when they come home.

Semper Fi.

March 14, 2006

The meeting of Iraq's first parliament session is Thursday, March 16, 2006; and the third anniversary of the war's birth is March 19, 2006. A letter from Kenton to his Dad arrived yesterday—his comments make me reach deep into God's Word this morning. I find relief in the book of Isaiah. His unit prepares for homecoming as another unit prepares to replace the 2/6 in the passing of the baton. Kenton mentions sacrifice of some who gave all and the hope that these dearly held brothers in arms and their deaths will count for something.

Isaiah 57:1,2
The righteous perish and no one ponders it in his heart; devout men are taken away and no one understands... Those who walk uprightly enter into peace; they find rest as they lie in death." The tears of so many, Lord. The tears of families on U.S. and Iraqi soil—innocence of children harmed and killed by terror, noble warriors who've given the ultimate sacrifice, families forever changed by these losses.

The battle before us looks so hopeless. Too many lives lost over these three long years. War and disillusionment. Resolve and justice. Mistakes and missions.

"Maintain justice and do what is right."
Isaiah 56:1,2

Your hand is over this mess, Lord. You do have everything in control despite the chaos that we see here with our natural eyes. Help my spirit eyes to be lifted up to You. Your ways are not my ways. Isaiah 55:8,9. Your ways are higher. Help me to be reminded of your higher purposes. You will accomplish what You desire and achieve the purposes which You desire.

"Maintain justice and do what is right."
Isaiah 56, 1,2

Not McRight. It's not quick and delivered in a throw away carton. To do what is right sometimes take time and much sacrifice. Pain is involved. I look at Your patience and resolve You exhibited in sending Your Son Jesus. Your patience with mankind. We killed Your Son, threw away the cross, and yet You still believe in us.

Isaiah 53:10,11 "Yet it was the Lord's will to crush him and cause him to suffer, and though the Lord makes his life a guilt offering, he will see his offspring and prolong his days, and the will of the Lord will prosper in his hand. After the suffering of his soul, he will see the light of life and be satisfied. By his knowledge my righteous servant will justify many and he will bear their iniquities."

You maintain Your justice to us. You will do what is right. We can count on that.

These memorials—these names of the lost—are never forgotten to You. Have mercy on us, God.

Isaiah 58:8-12 "Then your light will break forth like the dawn, and your healing will quickly appear; then your righteousness will go before you, and the glory of the Lord will be your rear guard. Then you will call, and the Lord will answer; you will cry for help, and he will say: here am I. If you do away with the yoke of oppression, with the pointing finger and malicious talk, and if you spend yourself on behalf of the hungry and satisfy the needs of the oppressed, then your light will rise in the darkness, and your night will become like the noonday. The Lord will guide you always; he will satisfy your needs in a sun-scorched land and will strengthen your frame. You will be like a well-watered garden like a spring whose waters never fail. Your people will rebuild the ancient ruins and will raise up the age-old foundations; you will be called Repairer of Broken Walls, Restorer of Streets with Dwellings."

Thank You for these words, Restorer of Broken Walls.

> DO JUSTICE
>   LOVE MERCY
>   WALK HUMBLY WITH THY GOD
>
> MICAH 6:8

March 16, 2006   Evening

I pulled into the Kroger parking lot that evening to pick up a loaf of bread. I noticed I was being followed closely by a large, shiny black truck. I pulled into the parking space and got out of my van to head into the store.

The young man in the shiny new truck also pulled in across from me, hopped out, and joined me in my stride. "Excuse me, ma'm," he said respectfully. "Are you a former Marine?" (The rear of my van carries the obvious USMC yellow ribbon, as well as a Marine symbol.)

"No," I laughed. "But my son is. He's in Iraq. You must be one too. I see the haircut." Strong shoulders and tall stance with a twinkle in his eyes, I could see the young man become relaxed. "What unit?" I told him the 2/6, and he readily offered "Lejeune. I'm a gunny from Michigan." We exchanged a few more tidbits of information, and he warmly took my hand and smiled again. "Tell him, 'Ooh rah!' for me, ma'm." as he shook my hand gently.

We both walked into Kroger's and on with our lives.

What a special group of guys! As I walked with him for just those few moments, I felt like I was walking next to my son.

You made my day, Gunny!!

March 19, 2006   8:20 p.m.

We just had the nicest surprise call from Kenton! He'd just gotten off guard watch and called to say their departure window date has been moved up to April 9-11. WOW! It's becoming more real. He peppered us with questions, "How was church? What'd Pastor Scott preach on?"

He said he still remembered the plane ride over and the apprehension he faced. Now it's time to get out of there. He was happy and satisfied with that.

I mentioned this being anniversary #3, and Kenton said it was just another day. We'll leave it up to the media and politicians to have their say.

I was talking to him, and he said he was about 15 feet from a burn barrel. Some shaving cream canister must have gone off, and the noise was loud over my end of the phone. I heard him say to a sergeant, "It's just the burn barrel, sir." I then asked if he'd had any close calls, and he said a few but couldn't really talk about it. He said if he never saw train stations or rail cars the rest of his life, that would be fine with him. I teased him about the rail cars on track in the yard behind my place of work at Kraft, and he laughingly said he'll probably have flash backs when he sees them!

He's assured me and Lenny it hasn't been that bad. Sometimes—even boring, he says. I said, "Boring is GOOD!" They're cleaning up the place since the new unit is coming in…getting rid of some "posters," he said. And he said he can't wait to see girls again!! Oh, boy, watch those raging 21-year-old hormones!

It's SO GOOD to hear him upbeat and optimistic about coming home.

March 30, 2006   8:30 p.m.

Well, I believe we're almost home free! According to Kenton's call, Friday, March 31, is his last day of combat. THANK YOU, LORD!!! From mid-September 2005 to March 2006: how many prayers? How many sleepless nights or interrupted sleep? How many nights of looking at the stars and wondering what Kenton was doing? I've lost count—thankfully! The beautiful spring weather unfolded today in Toledo, and my spirits felt hopeful and happy. I heard the birds actually singing when I came home this evening under a cool pink and blue sunset. The verse of "Amazing Grace" came across my consciousness today as a homecoming song.

"His grace has brought me safe thus far, and grace will lead me home." Grace is leading Kenton home, Father. How can I ever say "Thank You" enough times for Your protection and guidance while my son was in Fallujah, Iraq?

THANK YOU

    THANK YOU
      THANK YOU
        THANK YOU
          THANK YOU

Matthew 5: Blessed are those who mourn for they shall be comforted." My heart goes out to those families whose hearts are broken as their sons and daughters will not be on the plane home this April. Their sad journey home was already made. God, PLEASE comfort these broken-hearted families of those brave fallen warriors. Holy Spirit, wrap Your comfort around them and bring them peace and healing in due time. Please be with those children who now have lost parents. Father, You promised to be a father to the fatherless and to watch over the widow's border. Be mighty in that, dear God. Those kids need to know your fatherhood in a very special way. Walk beside those dear children who have tasted tears and grief in their tender years. They've had to grow up before the emotional coping equipment was fully installed. And that's tough sometimes. Bless them in hundreds of special, unique ways, Lord, over the course of their years for the pain with which they've learned to cope. Help them to know (in their heads) and feel (in their hearts) that You TREASURE them. And please give their parent in Heaven a hug from them.

"His grace has brought me safe thus far
And grace will bring me home.
　　　Amazing Grace,
　　　　　Lord, Thank You for Your
　　　　　Amazing Grace!
　　　　　　　Your daughter, Cathy

April 1, 2006　　　　　　6:30 a.m.

Spring storms passed through Ohio last night. The winds were strong and the lightning streaked through the black sky overhead. Katelyn and I stood outside in those winds as we waited for Lenny to pick us up. She huddled next to me, and I tried to assure her it was okay. Just a storm. But inside myself, I was rather thrilled by standing in the strong winds.

Job 37:1-24

At this my heart pounds and leaps from its place. Listen! Listen to the roar of his voice, to the rumbling that comes from his mouth, He unleashes his lightning beneath the whole heaven and sends it to the ends of the earth.

After that comes the sound of his roar; he thunders with his majestic voice. When his voice resounds, he holds nothing back. God's voice thunders in marvelous ways; he does great things beyond our understanding.

Each gust of wind pushed at our huddled backs. It was the touch of God in the winds. It was the sound of his voice in the thunder. It was bolts of lightning sent by His hand in the night sky. The spring storms signal a change. The earth begins to awaken. The buds are plump in the branches of the tree. The air smells fresh again. The birds' songs in the morning sound brighter and happier. The earth pushes forth new life in the tulips, crocus, and daffodils from the autumn's pregnant bulbs. We're ready for the earlier dawn and the sunset to come later—for the darkness of winter to pass away.

Thank You, Lord, for this change of seasons. It's more than a simple turning of the calendar. It's something I feel deep inside—this freshness in my spirit. I'm sure some of it is the nearness of Kenton's homecoming. We've been working on Kenton's homecoming banner. A Lejeune tradition for families to welcome their beloved warrior home from war. Families take tarps or a bed sheet (or even dixie cups!) and in large, bold letters spell out their messages to their Marine. Lenny and Katelyn designed our's for its place on the North Carolina highway leading into the military home base of the 2/6: Camp Lejeune in Jacksonville. We've gotten signatures from all walks of Kenton's life (school, work, friends, library), as well as sent messages from family in Illinois and Pennsylvania. It's quite cool to see all the wonderful signatures of support for him. How do we say "thank you" to all those who prayed and loved him and us through these seven months? And I am eternally most grateful to You, Father God, for this spring in the air and my step this April 1st.

April 8, 2006   5:00 a.m.

I was finishing up the last of the chores to be done before leaving work Friday night for our week of vacation. A few more emails, and I can close down shop for a week to ready ourselves to welcome Kenton home—at long last. Co-workers had wished us well for our trip to North Carolina. These loving friends who have listened to me for seven months as I watched at the gate for the news of our son and his 2/6. The road has been long. The miles wide between us. But Lenny and I continued to look down that road for our son. The light in the window has not gone out (well, maybe once or twice for a quick light bulb change!). Right before I shut down my computer, the phone rang. I didn't recognize this area code. And sure enough a pause and "Mom!" His voice sounded strong and sure. "I don't know how long his phone call will last, but I want you to know we're leaving Kuwait April 12 and we'll be home April 15 between 3 and 4 p.m."

The news we've long awaited has an arrival time. THANK YOU, LORD! Kenton told me about a welcoming ceremony at the field house, and I told him we'd already gotten a map off the website. "Great," he responded. "You have no idea how I can't wait to get home." He then went on to tell me what he'd been up to since they turned over operations on Sunday and gone to the "safe zone." He said they'd taken "unwinding classes" and done time with the chaplain at the base. The classes were good—taught him things he hadn't thought of. Life had been busy for them, but a chaplain's reminder that (especially for the married Marines) life had been busy for families at home as well. An exhortation to offer help at home for wives who'd carried the role of Dad and Mom to little children. God bless those wives of deployed Marines. Please keep those families intact and strong, Lord.

He lamented the fact that two of his good friends had gotten "Dear John" letters of news of broken relationships, and he said he was glad he broke up with a young woman a long while ago. He said it was tough on these guys to find out they'd been cheated on by their girlfriends. He wasn't sure of relationships when he got home, but he'd kept in touch with a few young women. He'd see how things worked out when he came home to Ohio. Lord, You know I'm always praying to bring the young woman who is best matched for him forward at the right time.

He continued on quickly saying there'd been a sandstorm two days ago, and he'd tried to take video in it so we could see what it was like. He had picked up stuff to bring home—some flyers he'd found in the street that he had no idea what it said, some dinare (Saddam money) and four rolls of photos. They'd done some precustoms inspections and were told "no sand home." He'd gotten a couple of Iraqi flags signed by his unit: one for former Marine Paul Norton (a Viet Nam vet). He said it was very important for him to give this to Paul—Marine to Marine. This is so touching to me—a generation of Marines apart—yet the baton is tossed from the Black Wall, Agent Orange, and the jungle to the sandstorms, mosques, and chaos of Iraq. It does mean something touchingly beautiful in the horror and pain of war to see this gesture. The brotherhood and its bond are strong.

Kenton was typically funny at the end of his call. "The other night in the hooch, I was in my rack and I started yelling because two huge camel spiders (the size of the top of a soda can) were coming at me. They were working like a team—with fangs!! I'll have nightmares of those things!!" I laughed and told him to check his bags and make sure he didn't bring any of those things with fangs home!!

April 13, 2006   7:30 a.m.

Psalm 121
I lift up my eyes to the hills
Where does my help come from?
My help comes from the Lord, the Maker of heaven and earth.

It is morning in Tennessee. I sit on our balcony at the motel and face a sunrise as it finishes its work on the foothills of the Smoky Mountains. The sky is pale blue with fluffy white clouds. Earth has awakened. The birds can be heard, the lavender trees are gorgeous, the tulips and daffodils have bloomed. The humans are also up and coming and going this early hour.

I am blessed. I am SO blessed. Thank You, dear Helper. Thank You, Maker of heaven and earth, for the beauty I've seen this week on vacation. The facets of the mountains in shades of green, lavender, smoky gray. The sunlight and shadows. The cleft rocks and mountain streams bubbling over and tumbling by the roadsides. The cool waters and majestic meadows. The buck and the deer feeding. The songs of the birds.

>I am blessed. I am blessed—so blessed.
>Thank You, Maker of heaven and earth.

April 14, 2006   10:30 p.m.

Everything is done for tomorrow's return of the 2/6. We're here in Jacksonville, North Carolina—the home of Camp Lejeune. It's so strange to be in this town without Kenton. It's so odd to walk past "high and tight" haircuts—hundreds of them—and not see Kenton.

I miss him. Can a parent be homesick for her kid? I wonder where he is tonight—on a plane flying home in the night's sky—somewhere, who knows where? Prayers for the final flight home for the last of the three groups of returning 2/6 heroes.

We drove down Marine Boulevard and saw all the homemade welcome signs. It's a wonderful tradition. Hundreds of "welcome home" messages along the highway entrance to Camp Lejeune. One creative miss spelled out "I love you, Earle" in huge strokes of Styrofoam paper cups! One "Miss you, Baby Boy." Another "The boys are back in town 2/6." Wonderful, lively "ooh-rahs" to the returning devil dogs of the 2/6. Ours is posted as well: Lenny and Katelyn's work of art along this highway of homecoming. We had friends and family sign it for Kenton—like a giant hug from all of us to him.

Yesterday, before we left Gatlinburg, I was browsing through a vintage Norman Rockwell picture book. One of the last pictures was Rockwell's "The Homecoming." My eyes filled with tears in the store as I stared at it. It came alive to me. I saw the back of the young soldier with his suitcase in hand and those who loved him threw their arms wide open to him. I saw his mother, at her doorway, in her red sweater and the look of absolute joy on her face, the blue star flag behind her on the door. The father and kids had wide smiles. Everyone stopped in their tracks as they realized he was home—SAFE. The neighbors peeking over, even the dog thrilled his boy was home. I choked up. It captured it all so well…the poignant moment of tender love and joy of a family whose beloved warrior is finally home.

Again, and Lenny and I've talked about this, we remember those families whose sons have given all—they don't get this privileged homecoming. Dear God, comfort those families of the fallen in the 2/6. What a sad time it must be this last night for them. Watch over their loved ones in a most special way, Lord. We honor these heroes as well and thank them for those who gave all.

April 15, 2006   10:00 a.m.

IT'S FINALLY YELLOW RIBBON DAY!!!

At breakfast, I talked to a New Jersey grandpa wearing a red "Welcome Home, Dave" tee shirt. His family of eight all dressed alike for his B-Company homecoming.

"Lots of prayers," Dave's grandfather says over coffee.

LOTS of prayers. Indeed.

April 15, 2006   10:00 p.m.

We unpack Kenton's things in the room of the Holiday Inn Express. Fine sand covers everything that he lifts from his sea bag. I open Kenton's Bible and smooth the pages that have become tussled in the trip home and feel the sand of Iraq on my palms.

A sigh…this is the sand from the ancient land of Abraham, Isaac, and Jacob…from Daniel…

April 21, 2006   4:00 a.m.

I work at a flour mill where we have these giant refrigerator-size wooden sifters. I've walked past them in the boiler room when they're out of service for repair. I could literally get inside and stand in this sifter—that's how large it is. And then, just like the sifter you hold in your hand when you're making a cake, I could shake and sift the flour through until all the impurities are out and it's winnowed pure and clean. Well, that describes somewhat what this last week of my life has been like. So many emotions and experiences that I feel truly "shaked, rattled, and rolled"!!

Emotions bubble to the surface fast and furious sometimes. Tears roll easily and unexpectedly. I'm not normally a crier; this week I've cried. Confusing and conflicting emotions pick at me sometimes. I need a day or two to process—to "sift" my feelings to get perspective. Here's some of what I remember most.

Saturday's Yellow Ribbon welcome home of the 2/6 was packed with emotion. The 2:00 p.m. homecoming was delayed until 4:00 p.m. Families milled around the gymnasium talking among ourselves—introducing one to another. We exchanged stories of our sons, asked their company, tried to see if we recalled hearing our Marine son's mention of their son. There were pictures of babies born during deployment in their pink and blue photo frames. The support group had set up pizza, Girl Scout cookies, donuts, pop, and cold water for all of us. We ate, talked, and waited in the warmth of the 80+ degree sunshine. An announcement by the CO of the Marine's buses arrival on Camp Lejeune and the trip to the Armory to drop off their weapons sent all of us outside to the parking lot to wait. The COs words to us: "Don't go looking for the Marines. They're on base. They will come. Allow them the dignity to arrive as a unit and to march in together. You and we've waited seven months. We can wait a little longer." OK!

Blue Star In My Window

Back in the gym and more meetings and stories. Tucked into the back corner of the gym was a memorial to the 12 lost Marines under the banner "Lost But Never Forgotten." Twelve beautifully done pencil-etched portraits of those Marines killed in Iraq from the 2/6. Kenton's Commanding Officer had sent a letter prior to his September 2005 deployment and mentioned no losses that period of time. This time it had been a staggering loss. I looked at these portraits and stood in line to sign the green velvet memorial books for each Marine. I wondered if Kenton knew any of these fine young men personally since there had been around 1000 in the city of Fallujah. I would learn later of LCpl. Jeriad P. Jacobs and Cpl. Brett L. Lundstrom. One young man came in a wheelchair to sign. Another blond young man stood next to the memorial book and bent over and sobbed. Raw emotions. I had to look away. The pain was so clearly evident of the price paid by these brave young Marines for this fledging freedom in Iraq. A blond Mom and I struck up a conversation. She sadly shook her head and said, "My son is in the Navy and is the corpsman. One of the fallen Marines came home with my son. I fed him French toast. My son called the night he was killed. He was one of the first to get to him. He was so upset. I can't believe he's gone." Our eyes connected and I could only lamely say," I can't even imagine what it must be like." These are the very ones I've prayed for, for whom I've searched the columns in *USA Today*. Now I'm face to face with their etchings and stories, and I'm speechless. I let the video camera sweep over the gym. I want to remember because the emotions are powerful to feel fully. We talk to parents and families of those whose this is a second or third deployment. "How long between each time?" I ask them. Not long, they respond.

The video of the 2/6 in Fallujah rolls on over and over as the music plays, "I'm Already There" by Lonestar. The song becomes drilled in my head those two hours of waiting. Finally, another announcement. "Let's go welcome our Marines home!" We all file outside again and secure a spot by the parking lot. The buses have pulled up at a distance. The Marines start filing out and march toward us. The music blares, sirens scream, people whoop and holler (me included!), flags wave, banners lift high and each unit moves steadily toward us. I dial Mom and Bill on the cell phone so they can take part long distance in the hoopla. Lenny spies Kenton first, but I don't see him. They all look alike to me!! They stop and the team leader tells them it's time for liberty.

"Chuh!" they shout back. They're released and suddenly this big, strong Marine in his desert cammies is in front of me. I hardly recognize him until I see those dimples. We embrace. My head is buried in his chest, and I know I hang on too long, but I feel his tight hug back and let go. I have to share him with Lenny and Katelyn! WOW! He looks SO GOOD! There is a grown up transformation. He's tanned and I notice his neck is bigger! Weird what Moms notice, I know. He explains, "Yea, Mom, I've been working out with weights." He looks fantastic!

We all hug again and head into the gym with all the other families.

The first place these returning warriors go to is to the back corner of the gym. Long lines wait to sign the memorial books. It is a slow process as they wait and then write. Hugs, stories in line, and handshakes. Lenny stands with Kenton in line. I go back to the tables and watch. I want distance from those emotions. It is too strong right now—too fresh. I want to allow them privacy for these few moments of reflection. Again, I wonder how these families of the fallen are? I almost feel guilty I am here and they are not. I learn, though, that one family has come. With a large number of people milling about, I have no idea who they are, but how brave they are. ROCK SOLID BRAVERY to face this sad homecoming for them.

We snap pictures, smile widely, make some introductions to my son's friends, snap more pictures, hug again. A few stories start to tumble out.

"It all changed after January 7th," Kenton said.

"I can't believe this is all for us."

And…"I can't believe we're home."

We gather our things, drive over to get his three heavy bags, shove them in the van, and he asks if I've brought him any of his clothes. DUH?! No, I never thought of it! I'm so sorry, son! What kind of mother am I anyway??!! He smiles and lets me off the hook. He can't go off base in these dirty cammies so we go to the Exchange and he quickly buys shorts, a striped golf shirt, and flip flops. As he pulls off his boots, I notice the odd shape of his ankles. Almost "Popeye"-like! He laughs at me and says, "Yea, Mom, I've had these boots on for seven months!" They've reshaped his legs! The flips flops reveal toes that have blisters. He could care less! Let's pay for this and get outta here! There are lots of Marines shopping for shoes and clothes. I'm not the only Marine Mom who forgot!

We pass a sign before exiting Camp Lejeune. "Be Important," it reads. Are they ever correct! As Lenny drives the van onto the highway, Kenton again says, "I can't believe this is ALL for us." Every banner on the highway shouts out its personal greeting to the 2/6. "The boys are back in town!" one white sheet shouts blowing gently in the wind of this sunny Easter weekend afternoon. He reads these signs, "I know him!" We pull over to the roadside and get out of the van for his giant signed welcome home "card." He's impressed by our sign: "Wow!" and "It must have taken you guys a long time to do this!" The smile is wide and the dimples deep. He's Home!

"I went 30 days with no shower. It's okay!" Smelling better, we head out to explore Jacksonville, North Carolina. He wants either TGIF salad bar or pizza. We end up at a Chinese restaurant. Whatever! It doesn't matter. We're a family of four again—finally. Stories start tumbling out about January 7th. Questions, answers, stories. It's now early evening. The air is refreshing, the sky bright blue in Jacksonville. We head back to the hotel for a lot of catching up and rest for he's tired. But, no—a quick trip to Wal-Mart where it's packed with other Marines. Boots, new 2/6 Marines on leave, and those nasty civilians! What a joy it is to be here at Wal-

Mart! Preparation for sleep comes early this Saturday evening. Kenton hooks up his laptop, congratulates us for getting the correct Seinfeld and Big Lebowski DVD sets, and makes a few calls to his friends. Only messages will do at this point because most of his friends are out and about this Saturday night before Easter. We turn off the lights and sleep.

Around 2:00 a.m. I wake up, and I see the soft light by his laptop. Kenton can't sleep anymore; he's still on Iraqi time. Lenny is also awake; and so in the dim light of a laptop computer, father, mother, and son sit on the floor of the Holiday Inn at 2:00 a.m. and begin to talk and listen to his stories of Fallujah.

April 2006 Weekend Homecoming

Driving home on Monday was an emotional purging time for me. We left Kenton in Jacksonville for his mandatory week at Camp Lejeune, and the three of us started the trip northward. I drove most of the time from North Carolina to Ohio. Lenny drove the first three hours and then we switched off. As Lenny and Katelyn slept, I found the tears began to slide down my cheeks. I needed to finally let go and release these pent up feelings. Seeing so much, being relieved of his safe return, seeing the depth of love for those lost, the simple joy of being a family of four at a table again—it was a lot to handle. So the tears came.

As we crossed into Virginia and West Virginia and the mountains moved ever so closer, the tears spilled out. No one knew in the car. I didn't need to talk.

Blue Star In My Window

I needed to cry. So I stared through the windshield at the fog, rain, and beautiful mountain countryside, set the cruise control on the van, and released the cruise control on my heart. When I pulled into our driveway in Ohio at 2:00 a.m., I felt tired and a little bit better. I would find the next few days tears would surface quickly from time to time. It was wonderful to be able to once again pick up the phone and call him. What a luxury the cell phone is! We arranged for his flight home and were able to TALK—no long lines, no faded out conversations. And lots of "I love yous"—so good to hear him.

On Thursday night, I called Kenton; and he was on his way to dinner with the Jacobs' family. He and several other Marines wanted to let Jacobs' family know what their son had meant to them—to give them some closure. Kenton's heart is touched deeply by feelings for these families of the fallen.

Saturday morning, Lenny, Katelyn, Mom and Dad, and I drove to Columbus, Ohio to pick up Kenton. He had flown into Columbus, spent the night at his best friend's house, and then we picked him up. I slid into the back seat of the van with Kenton, and the first thing he showed me was Lance Cpl. Jeriad Jacobs' memorial service bulletin. I saw a strong, young Marine, the only son of the parents. The only brother of these two sisters. It listed the pallbearers as the Marine Corps Honor Guard. My son bears him also in his heart. It was so evident this Sunday night as Pastor Tony Scott called Kenton up to the stage at the end of the church service (unexpectedly). He hesitantly went up to the front of the auditorium

Blue Star In My Window

when called. Pastor handed Kenton the microphone and asked him to say a few words. I knew Kenton was uncomfortable as I saw him run his hand over his jarhead haircut. And then he said, "It's kind of bittersweet . . . this homecoming. We didn't all come home. We lost six in our company. Please pray for these six families and remember them." Pastor Scott hugged Kenton and then did just that: prayed for those families.

When we walked out of the church, he was angry at himself for not saying all he wanted to say and for struggling with these strong emotions. But I was so proud of him. It shows true character to deflect from yourself to show what is really most important. Kenton knows the Lord brought him home this time. Everything is NOT neat, cut, and dry. There are still a lot of struggles ahead, I'm sure. But I was so proud of him tonight as he stood in the gap for the fallen brothers. The sunset was absolutely gorgeous as we drove home. Massive clouds in almost cylinder-like formation in pink, blue, and red almost. I told him, maybe God let Jacobs look down and see him being mentioned tonight in God's house. Kenton said, "I hope so. He deserved it."

It's time to put a cap on the weekend of return. From the flags and yellow ribbons on the fences, doors, and mailboxes as we drove up our street in the neighborhood that Saturday afternoon, to the strong hugs and tears of one Ramadi-deployed Marine Mom to this Fallujah Relieved Mom, to the conversation between Don of Viet Nam era and Kenton of Iraq era after the church service this morning—it has been a weekend of memories, for sure.

Following are the names of these six Marines who are true heroes. They taught my son what sacrifice is really all about.

Sgt. Josh Frazier
Cpl. Josh Snyder
Cpl. Brett Lundstrom
Cpl. Felipe Barbosa
LCpl. Jeriad Jacobs
PFC. Kyle Brown

April 27, 2006

Reconnecting is a good thing.

It's early Thursday morning, April 27 (my sister Shirley's #63 birthday). We're in lilac-lovely Illinois. The bushes are lush and heavy with their special floral scent. Yesterday's sky was blue and the sun shining. We had a wonderful Italian dinner at on Wednesday night with my old college friend Karen Diefendorf. After arriving at Lincoln Christian College's campus—the place Kurt and I met (Kenton's beginnings, I told him), I unexpectedly ran into Mr. Lynn Laughlin. Lynn spent a delightful hour or so with us talking to Kenton. He told my son that his Dad (Ernie Laughlin, a GREAT preacher at West Side Christian Church in Springfield, Illinois) and Kenton's grandfather (Virgil Dial, a beloved elder at West Side) were old hunting buddies—something I didn't know about my wonderful father-in-law #1. He reminisced with Kenton about his Dad and grandparents, we talked of times of the mid-70s as though they were yesterday. Many years, people, and time passages later, we still reconnected in a wonderful, hug-ending way.

Dinner at Guzzardo's with Karen was luscious as well. She thoroughly charmed Kenton, as I knew she would. Kenton had lots of time to bring out answers to her gentle, pointed questions. I sat back and watched a master Chaplain at work. But it was much more than just that. It was a servant of God who cared deeply and compassionately about a fellow soldier/marine. Stories tumbled from both chaplain/soldier and marine. Laughter, care, understanding. Much more understanding about his world than I would know, for sure.

When they talked of Jeriad Jacobs and Kenton relayed meeting with the family, Karen said something so beautiful and fitting. It was a Proverbs "apples of gold in settings of silver" moment! Kenton told Karen, "I just let his Mom know it was an honor to work with and know her son. We wanted to help bring some closure to his family. He was a true hero, and I wanted Jacobs' family to know I will NEVER forget their hero." Karen responded, "You know, Kenton, even Jesus on the night before He was crucified had dinner with his best friends and he told them to remember Him. The thief on the cross asked Jesus to remember him." Karen went on to remind Kenton and me that if God Himself—on that final night of His earthly life—found it important to be remembered, He as well as the thief on the cross thought it important to be remembered, and the stones in the cemetery lots cry out for remembrance—that this was one of man's most pressing desires: to be remembered. Our time here is so brief—some 9, 19, 90 years is what we're allotted. But we desire remembrance. "Remember me…" Kenton doesn't want to forget those now almost 2400 young lives sacrificed in this Iraqi conflict.

He played a song by Yellowcard entitled "Two Weeks From Twenty" for me while driving to Illinois about a young man who was close to his 20th birthday who became a soldier. The song bothered him in one particular line about a soldier signing away his right to be respected.

"That hacks me off, Mom! The rest of the song is okay, but that line is so wrong!" I told him those songwriters could never understand the true feelings of one who has been there. They may sing things that are politically correct, but unless they've been there, they'll never understand the deep respect warriors have one for another and for the honor of the job they do. A job well done, for the sleep they were deprived of, for the meals they missed, for the courage it took to do the jobs they did, for the horrible injuries so many now endure, for the lost times with family and friends, for the memories and sadness these young lives now bear—they have every right and reason to respect themselves for the mission they've borne and borne well.

April 28, 2006   10:00 a.m.

Our return to Ohio was around midnight last evening. The three days in Illinois were incredibly packed with "Kodak" moments and memories. Lincoln was great and the time there was well spent. The campus of Lincoln Christian College is thriving and contemporary, and I search for 30-year-old markers of the time I spent there. I looked at the buildings on campus and remember working in the Administration Building with a great staff of co-workers, fellowshipping in the cafeteria with friends where it didn't matter if it was "veal bird" or "beanza" night—trust me, you had to be there to appreciate those culinary disasters! Alumni Hall and my B-2 days where I was the 20-something young miss who never dreamed of one—let alone two—marriages to God-loving men with two wonderful children and scores of terrific times ahead. Like the Proverbs 31 gal, I want to "smile at the future" because the past has taught me there is much ahead to be appreciated. I think they call that "faith"!!

Wednesday's time with my two sisters, Mickey and Shirley, at Grand Prairie Mall in Peoria and the hugs of family that evening "on golden pond" at Lake Camelot at Gene and Shirley's home was wonderful, too. Kenton answered questions that I'm beginning to understand his answers after being with him. "What was it like, bro?" He talks of mission and the kids and the impact of the people there on his life. He'll say, "I wonder how the New England Reserve group is doing?" He talks more easily of Jacobs and

Lundstrom, massaging these events through his mind and mouth. He doesn't want pity. He wants people to know of the sacrifice still ongoing there. We run into a Barnes & Noble bookstore; and he's on a mission to show Mickey and me "<u>No True Glory</u>," a book by Bing West of the original battle for Fallujah. He pulls it out of the bottom shelf and opens to the map of Fallujah. His finger traces the north-south streets and the east-west streets. His base of operation is there and he runs his finger over it. It's like he's back there for a moment. He explains their movements to us, the areas of danger, and the worst areas of Fallujah. He snaps the book shut and wants to buy it, but shoves it back in its place and says he'll buy it later. We'll get it cheaper somewhere else . . . and we move on. The cigarettes come out, he smokes a quick one while we walk to the car.

Earlier on the drive on I69 between Fort Wayne and Indianapolis, we had stopped for gasoline. We stood outside the Dairy Queen: me eating a junior ice cream cone in the cold, 50-degree rain and he smoking his cigarette. We looked at each other—the first time I'd ever seen him smoke, sadly to say, and said, "Why are we both doing this destructive thing?" He then told me what it was like to smoke at night while in Fallujah—where he honed this detestable skill of smoking. "You don't want the enemy to see the red burn of the cigarette and watch the red glow from your mouth and head to your chest. They'd have a perfect target. So you cup with your hand and cover the cigarette when you bring it to your mouth so they can't see it." Chills run up my back, and it's not from the cold drizzle in which we stand. I pop the cone in my mouth and off we go on our drive southwest to Illinois.

Flashback to Gene and Shirley's house, I remember how Kenton plays with Ethan and

Olivia. Ethan, my great-nephew, is a five-year-old blond warrior on wheels equipped with a gun. He and four-year-old Olivia chase Kenton around Gene and Shirley's house, playing "soldier." The kids laugh with glee as Kenton falls down dead at their shots. It was only yesterday, I'm sure, when he and Aaron Mikolocyzk played the same commando games and painted their faces with camouflage markings of a soldier. I wonder what happened to Aaron?

Aaron & Kenton

Kenton was able to talk to his second cousin, 27-year-old Brad, stationed at Fort Bragg, North Carolina where he is in Green Beret training. Brad is a 7-year Army veteran of Afghanistan and Iraq. He counsels Kenton over the computer's video cam, and it is a good exchange from a sergeant to lance corporal. When Kenton expresses distress at misconceptions of the public on the war, Brad advises not to get too upset. "You can't let the fact that civilians don't understand get to you, dude." Brad counsels his cousin. It's sage advice from one seasoned warrior to this one whose not been in this game so long. The rules are sometimes fuzzy and everything not so cut and dry when you're in a game of urban combat with terrorists. And you know Round 1 is done, but Round 2 is just beyond the corner.

Kenton & Brad (Green Beret) in handshake

A lot of love packed into the 24 hours in Peoria, suitcases thrown in the car, and off to the Springfield area to meet up with Kenton's Uncle Klint. Such an odd, awkward feel to this reunion. We hadn't seen Klint since Aunt Lill's death in 1990. Thursday's reunion was stunning. Just seeing Klint as a humbled man who paid dearly for some mistakes softened my heart toward him. It was authentic remorse. God's grace toward the prodigal had been extended, and I dare not be the haughty "elder brother." As Klint came out to the car, greeting Kenton and me sincerely, I winced in my spirit. The build and voice so much like Kurt. Would this have been what Kurt's life would have been like had he lived? The gray hair, the slowed walk, the reliance on a walking stick...would this be ten times worse for Kurt who'd already lost eyesight, mobility, and his kidneys to the ravages of diabetes? I swallowed hard, thanking God that He mercifully took Kurt home—ready for his "new body" as Kurt so beautifully put it just days before his death in November 1989.

Kenton took to his old "new" uncle immediately. We only had two hours to accomplish the impossible—see three of the four cousins and have time to reconnect. Kenton and I'd prayed—eyes wide open—on the trip down to Springfield on I55 for His help in this mission. God was there and good to us. We were able to first meet Chad, Kenton's 24-year old cousin. Chad Edward and Kenton Edward—both named for their Godly grandpa Virgil Edward Dial. Chad was a grown up, sweet version of what I remembered. His soft, sweet slightly southern drawl reminded me of his dear Mom Gale. Kenton and Chad hit it off immediately. Chad had wanted to give Kenton a Marine knife he'd bought him, but it would have to be sent as we couldn't stay for a dinner. Chad then went back inside his place of employment (a carpet business) and bought out "cammie" floor mats for Kenton's new Honda Civic. What a kind, sweet gesture! The two cousins laughed incredulously when Kenton said, "Jeez, Louise…" and Chad exclaimed, "You say "Jeez, Louise?! No one else says that but me. People always laugh at me when I say that!" 17 years…Jeez, Louise!! It was meant to be. We take quick pictures, roll over to Lanphier High School for a 5-minute meet and greet with Klint's youngest son Evan. The poor 16-year old has no clue who we are, and we've probably embarrassed him in his freshman attendance office, but at least he's not in trouble he discovers as he's called down to the office mysteriously to meet these "strangers" from Ohio passing through town. More quick pictures and a marvel at how much Evan and Kenton resemble one another. Our last stop is an upscale bank in Springfield where 20-year old cousin Abbie Gale works as a teller (for 3 weeks). God had blessed us with NO CUSTOMERS at all at the bank so we rolled in and Abbie and Kenton met. These two, I believe, look most alike. Carbon copy faces on these cousins. Cute, bubbly Abbie in an apple green sweater stands next to her Marine cousin and they grin at one another. It's so cool seeing these two together! Quick hugs, they exchange phone numbers and we dash off again. A fast lunch at "Jolly Tamale" and Klint recalls family—now heaven's residents—and stories of the past. I ask him as we ready to leave, "What do you think Kurt would say?" "He'd be SO PROUD," Klint insists with a catch in his voice. So true! Klint gives his advice: don't smoke. The uncle gave his nephew two praise cds and an Oswald Chambers "<u>My Utmost for His Highest</u>" daily calendar. Kenton helps Klint carry his packages to his motel room. I watch them hug, and the lump in my throat is getting bigger. I wave as we drive away.

We stop at a gas station, and Kenton's frustration at having so little time here in Springfield erupts. "I feel like this is an unopened chapter in my life, Mom." He wants to stay and see how his cousins tick, meet the fourth cousin Eva who he planned to tease with memories of her Backstreet Boys obsessions, and enjoy the Dial-side of life. He determines to come back and see his four cousins before he deploys again. I break down in tears, as I tell him how I felt I was seeing an older version of Kurt in Klint and how tender Kenton was with Klint. Your Dad and the rest of the Dials (Grandpa and Grandma, Grandma Sally Best, and Aunt Lill) would be so proud of you, son. He grabbed my hand and held it for a time. It was a special day of surprises and prayers answered in a quick two hour package. He and I talked and reminisced over events. As midnight approached in our drive home, he called Abbie to thank her for the family time. It was a good, God-thing. Kurty, are you seeing us now?!

April 28, 2006   9:00 p.m.

I'm exhausted this Friday night. I fell asleep during "Oprah" (whom I love to watch on my vacation days) and have fought to continue moving all day. Kenton has worked his weights at Wildwood, ended a relationship with his first love for good, and had a date with another friend before driving three hours down to Ohio State University for a party with his high school buddies. I pray for safety for them all. What do 20-somethings do to party? I'm sure alcohol is involved. I never dreamed it would come to this. We didn't raise Kenton this way, never a drop of alcohol in our house, but the Marines sometimes have destroyed in 18 months what we tried to instill these past 20 years.

I have sadness about his changes in language, tobacco, and alcohol usage. He has relaxed in areas of addictive substances of alcohol and smoking. Lenny says he's shed tears over this. I have smelled it on him, seen him smoke now several times, tasted it in the car as we drove thought the night's highways, and stared at the stars. I told him last evening of how many nights I stared at the stars and moon and prayed protection over him and his unit—all the while thinking he was on the other side of that moon. Fighting boredom or fear, he picked up these habits which could be as deadly for him as a sniper's bullet—only not as quick. I pray he stops, as he says over and over he will. "I can quit anytime. I've done it before, Mom." I only pray he's correct on this.

Last Sunday's sermon by Pastor Tony Scott, nailed Kenton with four basic issues he had (and I suppose most 20-somethings in this generation have addressed for themselves). Returning home to Toledo from Columbus for his block leave with Grandpa and Grandma, Lenny, Katelyn, and myself Kenton had fired questions at us regarding the following:

1. Tobacco
2. Alcohol
3. Marijuana—legalizing it
4. Sex

It was as if, he said, Pastor Scott had a tape recording of our conversation from Columbus up I75 to Toledo.

> What's wrong with this stuff?! I still believe in Jesus—in God. But what if I need some of this stuff? I'm going back to Iraq. Why can't I indulge a little?

Long discussions, honest discussions, with all of his closest family chiming in. It was a verbal ping pong match. And then Pastor Scott addressed all four issues beautifully on the next Sunday morning. Do you think God pointed the arrow of His Word at this Marine? Oh, yea—and it was a perfect hit on the target. Pastor Scott talked on how the Lord created the vegetation on earth and told Adam and Eve to take dominion over it. Instead, the plants of tobacco, marijuana, corn and barley had been misused and taken dominion over man through the addictions that now have trapped mankind. Millions, billions spent and no cure for these addictions.

Grace extended, grace received is the only hope.

Monday, May 1, 2006

Kenton will visit two schools this week. Dutifully, because we're in such a time crunch, he'll carve out precious time to go to Katelyn's school and visit the fifth grade class which she attends just as he did prior to leaving in September 2005. He'll also go to Pittsburgh with Lenny on a visit with brother Bill's family and go to Bridgette's special needs class. Pennsylvania cousin Bridgette teaches special ed in a suburb of Pittsburgh. She had placed a picture of Kenton in her classroom. One young man had been very interested in Kenton. Bridgette had explained to her students that her cousin would be coming back from Iraq around Easter time. The young student had asked his teacher recently, "It's Easter. Where is 'that man' you said was coming?" Kenton, 'that man' would certainly etch time into his schedule to fulfill that promise just as he'd written them back answering their questions when they wrote him in Iraq.

Here are questions from Mrs. Gust's fifth grade class.

1. What was the best part of homecoming?
2. Were you exhausted?
3. What language do they speak?
4. Did you learn any of the language?

5. What is the Marines' nickname?
6. Did you get shot at? Hurt?
7. Were you nervous or scared?
8. Did you fight at all?
9. What did you do?
10. Did anyone you know get hurt?
11. What was the funniest part of being there?
12. What was the food like?
13. Were there surprises?
14. What was the scariest thing there?
15. Were you bored?
16. What's the difference between Iraq and us?

Tuesday, May 2, 2006   5:00 a.m.

We enjoyed our time at Highland with Mrs. Gust's fifth grade classroom. Miss Laura Kellogg (student teacher), Mrs. Keister, Principal Wiltse, Blade columnist Roberta deBoer, Lenny, and myself enjoyed listening and watching Lance Corporal Dial interact with these fifth graders. Kenton answered all their written questions (above) as well as the many raised hands and questions they peppered him with. He did it in an age-appropriate manner and was at ease before them. He gave them an accurate and clear account of a lance corporal's responsibilities in Iraq and brought them a perspective earned by being there. He asked them questions as well, "How many of you have Game Boys, DVDs, iPods?" Many of them raised their hands and he chuckled, "Jeez, I just got an iPod!" He then went on to tell the class of Mrs. Gust how blessed they were. On Christmas morning, he said, while on a city tour of Iraq, he thought of all the toys American children would receive. And he thought, in this Muslim country, there is no recognition of Christ's birth or the trappings upon which we've laid this holiday. We have—they have not. He tried to convey to them the blessings of a garbage man for the awesome job they do!! What a blessing to flip on a light switch, and the power comes on. Fallujah's power grid is unreliable. Garbage is burned and it is everywhere. He asked these young students how many had babies in their homes. Many raised their hands. He told them that areas smelled like a dirty diaper and that the trench with the brown water was an area you didn't want to step into. He talked about the clouds of flies that flew toward his face and mouth when one stepped inadvertently on garbage. He spoke of the camel spiders and the way they worked in teams, and laughingly drew a diagram of their teamwork on the chalkboard. Their movements seemed similar to the Marine's spider like movements in the city tours. Mrs. Gust later looked up "camel spiders" on the Internet, Katelyn told me... such a curious fiend these camel spiders were!

We are so spoiled and rich here. The basic necessities of life are eked out in 2/3rds of the world: clean water, food, rest, medicine, and clothing. Our cupboards and closets are cluttered; theirs are empty. Does this give me some insight into how the rest of the world looks at us: U.S.? We are smug, obese, cluttered, prideful, and profane. No wonder so many hate us. Wouldn't I be the same if I, as a hungry child with tattered clothes, looked through a cold window at the stuffed-full toy shop of America? If I saw food piled high and decayed, discarded things tossed aside that I so desired and dreamed of?

Wouldn't I?

Friday, May 5, 2006   5:30 p.m.

This afternoon, in a corner of a restaurant, in a 4-person booth, there was a private exchange of admiration and respect between two Marines. This was a meeting of a father/son of sorts. Today, the water from the rains of Viet Nam and the oil from under the sands of Iraq flowed together. Water and oil don't usually mix; however, today they merged and flowed in unison. Let me tell you about it.

The appointment was made on a long distance call from Iraq from the 21 year old lance corporal to a 50-something lance corporal in Oregon, Ohio. A future date was set. The two Marines, accompanied by the wife of one and mother of the younger, shook hands. The younger lance corporal pulled out an Iraqi Freedom flag, which had been signed by his company in Fallujah and presented this flag to the Viet Nam veteran. Words of honor and respect were said. The Viet Nam veteran cradled the flag to himself, his face showed the strain of the past 35 years, and a tiny tear popped out from the corner of his eye. At first there were few words. Sometimes, no words are necessary when emotions run this deep. The wife and mother exchanged glances, and both almost felt guilty about being present at this intimate moment. But both were glad they stayed. For what next took place was truly remarkable.

The young man excused himself from the table for a few minutes. While he was away, the older man pointed to the empty seat and said, "That was me 35 years ago." When the young man returned, the two began to talk and question one another. They had a language of their own, punctuated and peppered by abbreviations and numbers that a civilian would not understand. It was the washing of time from the older man's face that I noticed since I was on the opposite side of the table from him. The tears would gently roll down his cheeks as he knowingly shook his head while listening to the younger man's stories of Fallujah. The younger man's voice took on a quicker pace as he explained situations that were so strikingly similar. Stories poured out of both of them. They locked eyes as they talked. One went from boot camp to Okinawa and onto Viet Nam. After a time, he was hurt grievously and immediately flown out of Viet Nam and spent 5 months in a VA hospital. He was separated from his brothers, and he felt the sting of that separation. He knew what to do there; he didn't know what to do in this civilian world.

The younger one was fresh from boot camp and School of Infantry then flown into Fallujah. He talked of walking past the "Blackwater Bridge" each day where on March 31, 2004, four Americans were burned and hung out to be mocked by many in the city of Fallujah. They both talked of snipers, of that single shot, and the coward's escape. They both talked of the innocent families who, simply by being born there at that time in history, were living in hell on earth. They talked of children who were abused and used by an enemy to throw grenades for the reward of a toy. They talked about their rifles. They talked about those who didn't make it home. They talked of an empty mattress of a fallen comrade. The younger talked of meeting with family members of the fallen and conveying to the family what a privilege it was to serve with their hero. The older Marine talked of the loss of so many brothers who now are dying daily from The Agent.

They each wondered if we had learned any lessons? They winced at the thought that maybe it was all for nothing after all.

The wife and mother said little. How could we? A father and son were being born. A father from the generation of the jungle stood watch over the son from the sands of the desert. It was time for the two women to depart and leave this union.

Before the meeting, the younger man told his mother of his intentions in this meeting. He wanted to honor and thank this man for his courage and thank him for the job he had done those many years ago. His fellow brothers joined him in this by their signatures on the flag for this hero from Viet Nam.

After the meeting, the older man called his wife and said, "This is the closest I've been to a hero in my whole life. He's the cream of our youth."

They posed for a picture before they departed that afternoon in the parking lot. Arms were flung around each other and both were holding onto the edge of the flag. Two lance corporals linking arms through the years and tears of life.

Psalm 127:3-5

**Sons are a heritage from the LORD,
Children a reward from him.
Like arrows in the hands of a warrior
Are sons born in one's youth.
Blessed is the man
Whose quiver is full of them.
They will not be put to shame
When they contend with their enemies in the gate.**

Kenton with veteran Paul Norton, USMC, holding Iraqi flag

May 6, 2006   5:45 a.m.

It is the last night that four sleep under our roof. Kenton will leave early this morning to drive south to

Jacksonville, North Carolina in his newly purchased Honda Civic. He's so proud of that car purchase from his Iraq earnings. He put 2500 miles on it in just over a week while on leave. Trips to Illinois and Pennsylvania, as well as Columbus, for important family visits and reconnections to loved family and friends in Ohio. The two weeks have flown by...I hardly believe it's time for him to leave again.

I've so enjoyed his pop-in visits at home and work. He was never home for long! I enjoyed smelling his cologne again, seeing the trash pile up around his bedroom, doing his laundry, seeing his car parked outside when I come down the stairs in the morning. I LOVED the long talks. Seven months of static on a phone line will help you truly appreciate the facial expressions, wit, and conversation from this Marine son. He hugged me on his last night and said, "It's going to be okay, Ma." before going out for a last tackle session in our backyard with our dog Joey. Joey sat on his foot—like he did before—this dog's way of saying, "STAY!"

I wish he could, but then he wouldn't be LCpl. Dial, Kenton E. He's got to go.

Our home is blessed by God for its fullness this last night.

May 11, 2006

I pledge
Allegiance
To the flag
Of the United States of America

How many times have I made that pledge? We started our school days with our hands over our hearts.

My hand has been over my heart these past seven months, Lord.

And to the Republic
For which it stands
One nation under God
Indivisible

I gave the best I had to this land.

Our sons and daughters—the very best we have to offer in allegiance to our country.

So many military families who have given their best.

With liberty
And justice
For all.

May 22, 2006   10:20 p.m.

The light still burns brightly in my window tonight under the blue star. He's back home for a month now. My son has returned from Iraq—safely, soundly.

I know—I KNOW—I am blessed in this.

Some have lost their young men and women. Daily I've watched the death count rise in **USA Today**. I've whispered silent prayers of comfort for the families— the wives and children, Moms and Dads, brothers and sisters of these fallen heroes. I've also said prayers for the Iraqis as I've seen pictures of their huge losses. Innocent victims of war. My heart goes out to those wounded and forever scared by this war—for each one of us has been touched in some measure. Some truly have paid a high price. I remember meeting a beautiful Iraqi woman and her husband last week—owners of a local business. They have lived in the United States for the past ten years. We'd been asked to bring some of Kenton's Iraqi items (money, pamphlets from the city tours he'd done, a first grade instruction book from a mosque he'd found, some pictures, and an Iraqi flag) to a restaurant so "Anne" could see them. As she looked at these items, her lovely eyes filled with tears as she told us what the Arabic words said. She looked away and said, "It's hard. I still have family there. It could be so beautiful."

Good, kind, loving people on both sides of war—separated by an insurgency and snakes of cowardice and hatred. Dear God, please bring justice to those who plot evil and death to the innocent.

My son made a comment to me about a raid on one house in Fallujah. The women in the house stood begging Kenton (as the second Marine into their home). One held her Qur'an in front of her as a shield and begged Kenton, "No, mister, no!" Kenton said, "Mom, she looked at me like I was Satan. Something terrible must have happened to her before." In the past three years, between the 1st Exped. Force and 2nd Exped. Force in Fallujah, only God knows and sees what has taken place in these homes to these Iraqi families. His heart must certainly break as He watches over us.

We war in our hearts—the battle rages on. While this one war—yet another war in the list of history—

continues on and (hopefully) closes soon, there will most certainly be more to come. What looms on the horizon? Iran next? As a mother of a Marine, I shudder at that notion; however, I'm certain there will be more. The battles are not done. Only when Jesus returns will true peace exist.

"No shalom, no shalom" is what Johnny Cash's "When The Man Comes Around" says. Johnny, you were right.

So, for my Marine son, my God, I ask for his and all other military brothers and sisters safety and protection. I pray You strengthen their inner selves and bring them to a saving knowledge of You, Lord. I pray these experiences they've had will drop them down to their knees in honor of You. I pray that no bitterness take root in their hearts. I pray for gratitude to spring from deep inside to You for walking with them through these muddy streets, desert sands, and shadows of death they've faced. I pray those beloved ones they've lost will always be remembered for being the heroes they truly are. I pray for the children, spouses, and families of those fallen, Lord. Please comfort them as only You can. Wide arms of mercy, surround these families of the fallen, Lord. May we never forget their sacrifice for freedom's sake. Be with the children especially, Lord. They've lost so much in their tender years. Be a father to the fatherless and a husband to the widow, and watch over the widow's borders, as you promised in your Holy Scripture. Forgive us and them where we've failed. Help us in this imperfect world to get along better. Draw us to Your purposes, Father. Draw us nearer to You, for only You are perfection. We can simply reflect your grace, love, and mercy one to another when we draw near to You. Guide our leaders and speak wisdom to them, Father God. (Proverbs 24:6) God of infinite order, bring peace to our chaos. Help us to trust You during times of trial and when we come under attack, help us to hold up our shield of faith. Equip us to do Your work, Lord, while we still have time. The days draw short. The night is coming. Help us to look for your Light.

Amen

I am the light of the world...
JESUS

Memorial Day 2006   David's Mighty Men

"These are the names of David's mighty men: Josheb-Basshebeth, was chief of the Three, he raised his spear against 800 men, whom he killed in one encounter. Next to him was Eleazar, he was with David as he taunted the Philistines gathered at Pas Dammin for battle. Then the men of Israel retreated, but he stood his ground and struck down the Philistines till his hand grew tired and froze to the sword. The LORD brought about a great victory that day...Next to him was Shammah...took his stand in the middle of the field. He defended it and struck the Philistines down, and the LORD brought about a great victory.

During harvest time, three of the thirty chief men came down to David at the cave of Adullam, while a band of Philistines was encamped in the Valley of Rephaim. At that time David was in the stronghold, and the Philistine garrison was at Bethlehem. David longed for water and said, "Oh, that someone would get me a drink of water from the well near the gate of Bethlehem!" So the three mighty men broke through the Philistine lines, drew water from the well near the gate of Bethlehem and carried it back to David. But he refused to drink it; instead, he poured it out before the LORD. 'Far be it from me, O LORD, to do this!' he said. 'Is it not the blood of men who went at the risk of their lives?' And David would not drink it."

Bethlehem was home to David, son of Jesse. And David longed for water.

David was in a Philistine stronghold, in the caves of Adullam. There was no comfort here. They had been in the caves for some time; one night would be enough for me. But they stayed encamped here.

David longed for something of home. A simple drink of water and the water from home. He wanted that which was familiar and life sustaining. He knew exactly where it was: that one thing he wanted. He could see it in his mind's eye. The gate—the well—near beloved Bethlehem—that thirst quenching water from home—where the enemy Philistines' garrison was.

And these three men—"Josh, El, and Sham"—men who'd banded together with David, men who volunteered willingly to go with him through hardship, battle, hell itself if necessary, saw the longing for that water from home. These men had come to

David broke, busted, and some depressed (I Samuel 22:1,2). David had accepted these misfits and had poured himself into them; and they, in time, had become David's mighty men. They saw the longing of their leader and said, "We'll go get it for him." No job so insignificant it would not be done.

> Kick down a door—do it.
> Mentally prepared.
> Go behind enemy lines—do it.
> Defy common sense.
> Call on courage—go do it.
> Thigh against thigh in the thick—like the men at Iwo Jima supporting the flag.
> Bodies pushed against one another to assess and overcome.
> No sacrifice—no thought of sacrifice too great.
> Though indeed the sacrifice WAS great.
> Silent heroes just doing their job.
> Completing the task.
> Bringing water from home.

Water from the shores of the Atlantic and the Pacific. Muddy Mississippi water, Great Lakes droplets, Rio Grande gorges, mountain streams, Louisiana bayous, islands and inlets. All flowing water of cool freedom from coast to coast. All to quench the thirst.

Water—can't live without it. Refreshing water from home. Freedom, like water, we who have tasted it, can't live without it. It's life-giving and nourishes. And sacrifice is required to bring that from home in a dry land that has thirsted long and hard in this arid desert under a dictator who only allowed a trickle to pass through. Cruel terrorists who would give all to stop the flow of freedom in this desert and would extend their hate to these shores if this vigilance did not prevail.

These warriors—Josh, El, and Sham—broke through enemy lines, drew water from the well, and carried this precious gift back to David. David saw all they had risked for his request, refused to drink it, and instead, poured it out before the LORD as an offering. He saw those who'd given all and could not bring himself to waste their sacrifice. "Is it not the blood of men who went at the risk of their lives?"

David was a leader who asked something hard of his mighty men. Did David know the cost to his men for this request? Did the leader know fully what it would require? Did the three mighty men flinch or cower in the request of David? No, these warriors broke through, did what their leader asked, and secured the request of their leader.

The water from home was placed before this leader David. David, seeing their sacrifice and valor, was touched so deeply by their courage, honor, and commitment to him that he could not/would not drink this sacred cup. These men who risked their lives for their leader—for his call to arms—now stood tall before David. And David, the future King Leader, took their cup of sacrifice and poured it out before the LORD as an offering.

In the same way, do these king leaders of all wars fully realize the sacrifice of their mighty warriors?

No man—king leader or otherwise—can truly appreciate the sacrifice. But GREAT leaders treat the cup of sacrifice of their mighty warriors in a sacred way and pour out their hearts and souls in prayers to the LORD, in the same manner as David, before these flag-draped coffins.

From the wars of yesteryear to the jungles of the 60s and 70s to the deserts of today, sacrifice calls from monuments, black Walls, and fresh graves of mighty men and women of this generation.

May our leaders, and we as a nation, realize the cost of the cup and never forget the sacrifice of those mighty warriors who responded to the call.

August 7, 2006

Almost a year now since this journey began in earnest, and three months since Kenton's return from Fallujah. The sifting time still goes on somewhat. Things are not as they were before. While I'm eternally grateful for his safe return, I sometimes wonder where the young Kenton went. A matured son returned, and he is certainly different. I see him on "fast forward" mode these days. He's pushing hard to experience all he can before deployment #2 in March 2007. There's an edge to him now, a raw cutting edge at times. The outside Marine moves quickly, decisively, and rarely stopping at any one spot too long. He's not afraid to speak his mind or use his fist, if need be. He returned on a mission to find a lady love, and he accomplished that quickly. He's made some decisions I consider foolish and even sinful, yet he offers no excuses or apologies. It is what it is, per the Marine, and it's none of your business. I shall forever blame the USMC for taking away my child and returning this man-son I find hard to recognize at times. The war certainly changed him. While there are tender exchanges at times and more hugs and quick kisses on the cheek for his Mom, there is defensiveness and a wall hard to scale at times. He is an adult now, he tells me over and over. He can take care of himself, and I know that's true. But I still like it when he brings his dirty laundry home, and I can at least do that for him.

He's returned, but he's going back. So he's not returned truly. He's "on hold," high and tight, and that describes more than a haircut these days. No, not high on drugs—though it sounds as though many returning soldiers and Marines do "pop" on their drug tests. What I see is more of a distance—an unwillingness to enter his old, innocent life and an arm's length distance to the old ways. While there are days he hates the Corps and counts 900+ days until he's finished with it, I wonder how he'll cope fully back in civilian life. It's a love/hate relationship with the USMC at this point, I gather. The Corps has turned him into the man he wants to be, and sometimes he struggles with that man, I think.

They come. They go. This class of cammie clad charged up batteries. We expect them to be there, face situations the most mature of us would run screaming the other way, and yet they go day after day, deployment after deployment, now year after year.

They train.
They go.
That's the way it is.

August 22, 2006   1:40 A.M.

And so now my son has returned from war in Iraq. Four months have passed . . . almost a season now he's been home. I thank God he's home. I know we're blessed he's returned. But just as seasons bring change . . . subtle changes at first . . . then later stronger currents of change to draw you into a new season . . . in the same way Kenton has changed.

When he was a small boy, maybe 2 or 3 years of age, I used to take his hand to walk and try to keep track of this small mound of energy I had been given. He would hold my hand for a bit, but I could always feel this small hand begin to twist and pull away from me. He hated to hold my hand. He wanted to be free of my clasp and walk/run/charge ahead of me. So I would let him run ahead of me and yell out to him, "Kenton, slow down." Or, "Son, stop at the corner and wait." Some of the time he listened to me, and some of the time he did not. We had a thing with Kenton. Our minister, Jim Platner, started it. Jim would get down eyeball to eyeball with Kenton and would say to this 5-year old charge of a boy, "Kenton, look me in the eyes. I'm talking to you." He'd focus in on the adult for awhile, maybe get the point we were making, and then go on his way. I can't count the amount of times I said to him, "Kenton, look me in the eyes. I'm talking to you."

Blue Star In My Window

I planted everything I knew into this son of mine. I sincerely tried to give him every good seed I could find and afford. I prayed, laughed, cried, disciplined, let loose, pulled in, let go, released, took back, threw my hands up, and started the whole process over and over again throughout the years. I gave it all I had and enjoyed every second of raising this boy. He was and is my "joy boy." Always will be. I love him with all my heart.

Sometimes I wonder where he went. A young man returned from war in Iraq, and sometimes I don't know this young man. The softness is gone. The cammies now cover a young man with broader shoulders and a thicker neck. He's proud of that; and he's worked hard to achieve this strength. He's sharper around the edges now. Decisions seem to come totally independent of his family now. He makes his decisions and lives with them. The Marines have done their job. I have done my job. And somewhere in between of that is my son.

I am learning to know this young man who, it seems to me, now lives in fast forward mode. He has very little time now for me. And that's okay. I admit I have been jealous of his time away with friends and new lady love; however, my head tells me this is as it must and should be. I remember longing to be free of my home when I was in my 20s. Once I left for college, I forever left that home on Gulf Stream. I never went back but to visit. It's the same way now for Kenton. He'll never come back but to visit briefly. He's made his way into the world and traveled thousands of miles from home both physically and emotionally. He's secure and lives his own life now, and he's not afraid to let me know that.

When we disagree on aspects of life, he speaks his mind. He makes his decisions and his mistakes and agrees to live by his decisions and missteps. He tells me it's now none of my business when our paths diverge one from the other. The line in the sand has been drawn. I am proud of the noble work he's accomplished in Iraq and am proud of him. And while I totally disagree with portions of his life now chosen, I must now only watch as my prodigal son goes along his path. I now stay home and watch down the road for him to return someday. I pray the scripture over and over, "Train up a child in the way he should go; and when he is old, he will not depart from it." My tears and prayers are seen by the Father. My son has no use for tears, but he still thanks me for praying for him. He is now hardened to that which I hold dear. He tells me, "Mom, I still have my faith." But it's being chiseled out in a much different lifestyle than that which we have raised him. We have lectured him on the evils of smoking, drinking, crude language, sexual temptations. His terms with God are different from mine. I pray for him to return to the values we've taught him.

What of this generation, God? They're so different, as I'm sure each generation is. But the sewage of the media has seeped into their psyche. I'll call it "cafeteria God." They now pick and choose the parts they want to believe. They question everything. They blind themselves to caution and embrace risks and heresies. And they hang onto their thread of faith and say, "We'll get back to that." I pray there's time. Because in this fast forward mode, maybe there won't be time. Kenton tells me, "Mom, I want to experience all of life before I go back to Iraq in March. I don't know if I'll be back. Jacobs thought he was coming back. And he didn't get that chance. So I want to have every chance I can to get to do what I want to do before I go."

We yell at one another. I tell him he's wrong to think this way, and I mince no words in telling him he's living in sin. I remind him, "God has children; He has no grandchildren." He can't piggyback on my faith. It must be between God and Kenton. I email him, he emails me. We don't speak for days. He tells me it's none of my business. I need to stay out of it. So I'm trying to learn. Sometimes the emotional/spiritual distance between us is now greater than the 8000 miles of physical distance that was there when he was in Iraq. This compliant kid who gave us absolutely no trouble at all growing up is now long gone and in his place is a young man who speaks his mind and lives life on his own terms. I still love him dearly. I'm his Mom. He will always be my son.

But I must relinquish him to the Father. My God/his God. I know he still has faith. And Jesus tells me if there is even a mustard seed worth of faith . . . there's hope. My job of parenting him is over. My joy of loving him will never be done. Like the prodigal's Father, I stand at the end of the road and watch for his return. I can remember my Mom standing at her doorway watching me pull into the driveway each time I came home. My husband tells the story of his grandmother knowing her son's footsteps on their porch when he returned from war, "Wilbert, is that you?" We parents will always watch for our children to come home . . . if ever so briefly.

There is still a blue star in my window. And under the blue star there is a light. That light has now burned through many bulbs. It won't go out until his service to our country is complete. I pray for all our blue stars . . . our sons and our daughters. Many have been replaced by gold stars. And I pray for those families who have sacrificed all for this country. I pray that this light of Your love, Heavenly Father, leads them home.

Carry us Home to you, Father of all. For we have *ALL* been prodigals at times in our lives. And we prodigal children need to know we can still come Home.

October 1, 2006

They come. They go. It's ebb and flow like an ocean tide moving in and out. One group returns while another bears the brunt of the new responsibilities in the war. This class of cammie clad, charged up batteries that the politicians in Washington move in and out on the chessboard of public opinion and strategic decision-making policies. They're nameless faces of troops arrayed in checkered brown and tan uniforms, sunglasses hiding their eyes. We expect them to be there, face situations that the most mature of us would run screaming the other way, and yet they go day after day, now year after year. They train

Blue Star In My Window

relentlessly. They get bored and frustrated. They stay motivated and grow slack sometimes. They're spit and polish Marines sometimes, lazy and foolish other times. And they're field Marines who give 100% when they're called upon.

This is the Class of Post 9/11. They're the soldiers, Marines, sailors, and airmen who joined after that bright blue-skied September day of disaster. I remember the afternoon of September 11, 2001, stopping by the Kroger's where Kenton worked after high school just to touch base with him. He was bagging groceries, and I looked at him and knew his time was coming. He was already in the delayed entry program of the USMC. I asked him what he thought. He said, "Mom, I'd go tomorrow if they'd let me."

These guys and gals knew what had happened. They'd watched it on the news over and over, and a deep resolve came over this generation. It was their time. It was their place. It was their chance to make a difference. They knowingly took the oath to protect the United States of America. Innocently, yet determinedly, they stared down the pathways of their future lives and signed up.

Tom Brokow wrote a best selling book, "The Greatest Generation" about the World War II era. I wholehearted believe that generation of warriors deserves every accolade we can give them. My own Dad was a WWII and Korean War vet. He, and his fellow brothers in arms, paid dearly. The Viet Nam vets paid a different kind of price. They, too, deserve our love and respect for the pain they're carried and the thankless job they did.

But this Class of Post 9/11...they're a special breed also. And I believe them to be a new "greatest generation." Not just because my son is one of them. But because of the resolve, fortitude, and pure guts it takes to go up against a nameless terrorist and try to make a difference.

There are now almost 3000 fallen heroes. I heard on the news the other day that the body count for Iraq and Afghanistan almost equals those who perished on 9/11/01. It's as if the Twin Towers' mirrored image of those who died in the fiery blast now faces another Tower from Babel of those who have laid down their lives to go after that enemy who confused and destroyed that day.

This Class of Post 9/11, these military troops, are in the hardest school in the world. Kenton's friends enter their senior year in college this year. My son enters his second deployment to Iraq in 2007. Many have done 2, 3, even 4 tours or duty in these dry desert sands. What kind of payback will the world give them for time in the school of the sandbox they've endured?

Dear God, I pray for each of them. For the men and women they are becoming. For the difference they ARE making.

These who were our babies in the 80s are now the mission-minded men and women of these troubling, unsettling times.

This is our newest Greatest Generation.

February 4, 2007   4:30 p.m.

My mother-in-law (who has the perfectly coiffured home inside and out—car included!) recently gave me an article from her AARP magazine on clutter. Now some may think that's a double insult OR a reality check, as I am of the AARP generation and I do exist in a world of clutter. I think I like existing among the memories of things past while I hurl through my present existence.

But I do find it hard to discard. I have things in my closets that mean something to me because of whom it represents or who gave it to me. One such reminder of the past has been on the far side of my closet for nearly 20 years. Yet today, I pulled it down—so glad I never gave it away. It's zero degrees outside this sunny Sunday afternoon. I look out the window and you'd never guess its wind chill of -23 degrees is dangerous to man and beast. And it's the perfect afternoon for a closely knit peach and salmon colored afghan given many years ago from Kenton's Aunt Lillian Tomlinson.

Aunt Lill—now there's a name from the past. She was a chain smoking, divorced, fire ball from my first husband's side of the family. The first time my (then) boyfriend introduced me to her in the 70s, she had just returned from a trip to Las Vegas with her girlfriends. She worked full-time, had a stylish head of silvery gray hair, wore a size 12, and loved to give you her opinion on any subject that came up. The years of smoking had given her a growly sound to her voice, yet she had a quick smile and wit when she approved of you. And she wasn't afraid of letting you know her disapproval with a cigarette dangling from her mouth if the situation warranted.

But she loved her nephew Kurt Dial—who was to become my first husband—with a fierceness and tenderness seldom seen between aunt and nephew. And when our son Kenton was born many years later in 1984, that loved transferred generously to that great nephew.

Aunt Lill and Kenton would playfully argue when he was a five year old boy. He pestered her to quit smoking. Her comeback was, "When you quit sucking your thumb at night, I'll quit smoking!" Kenton did learn to fall asleep without his thumb when he was a bit older at 8, and beloved Aunt Lill died of lung cancer in 1990.

So 17 years later, I pull out an afghan from my cluttered closet and give it to my Marine son as a keepsake from his childhood while he's home on his block leave. It will keep him warm with memories of Aunt Lill and her spunk, wit, and pure pluck—which her great nephew inherited, I think.

February 4, 2007　　　　　　　　Later in the day

"Mom, I brought you a present," he said as he came through the door on the first day home that weekend. And in he walked, broad smile, and an overflowing hamper of dirty, smelly clothes. Now this could be any twenty-something young man home from college or a quick trip home from a big city job.

Blue Star In My Window

But the dirty clothes in this hamper contained desert cammies with sand still in the pockets. It never quite goes away, he says, with his dry wit. I was never good at checking his pockets figuring they'd been emptied earlier. I was wrong as a lone AA battery clunked in the dryer. Reaching into the pocket to retrieve the noisy offender, I pulled out a short cigarette butt and a small piece of paper folded over several times. Sand covered the page torn from a notebook during desert training in California. And what I saw caused me to pause and lean against the washing machine.

In my son's handwriting are the words of war: English phrases and their Iraqi pronunciation. Words like:

Slow down.
Stop.
Get out of the car.
Open door.
Open trunk.
Open hood.
Come with me.
I need to search you.
Hands up.
ID
Do you have a weapon?
Wait here.
Here's your stuff.
Drop your weapon.
Terrorist.

I close my eyes and shudder. I've just glimpsed into the reality of his job. All written down on a paper smaller than his iPod. Doing his laundry, folding his green tee shirts, hanging his digitized cammies on hangers in my basement—all reminders of his redeployment next month.

I ask him what he thinks of those who support the troops and oppose the war? I'm confused by this. But it's a no brainer for him.

"They can think whatever they want. It's not going to change the fact that I'm leaving in thirty days. That's what makes this country so great! We can all think what we want."

Sometimes I've taught my son.

And sometimes my son teaches me.

MUTED SACRIFICE

I'm sorry, but I wasn't listening...

~~To the politician who sees this war as a strategy for success or failure in this campaign or political record.

~~To the news organization that only sees the negative story line in all the headlines that are to be printed and ignores the positive things our troops have accomplished.

~~To the shrill cry of horror as the Iraqi woman sees the explosion which takes her beloved's life.

~~To the extremist who never seems to tire in his thirst for blood and sees innocent men, women, and children as unfortunate collateral damage in his jihad.

~~To Osama bin Laden who extols the glory of martyrdom to his followers.

~~To the cry in the night of a woman who grieves over her loved one lost from the two towers or in this struggle for enduring freedom on a foreign soil.

~~To the stooped, silver veteran whose heart hurts as he salutes yet another fallen young warrior.

~~To the young soldier in his or her cammies as he/she talks on his/her cell phone in a nameless airport terminal on his/her busy way here or there.

~~To the young child as she asks her tired widowed mother, "When is Daddy coming home?" for the umpteenth time.

~~To the wife as she wonders, "How many more days until I see him again?"

~~To the flag as it snaps in the breeze at half mast.

I'm sorry, but I wasn't listening for a moment.

The noisy blare of the world was silenced as I watched the young soldier in his green Army dress uniform slowly approach the flag draped oak coffin of the freshly fallen sergeant from his unit. The moment was powerful. Unashamedly he wiped away his tears. He held in his hands his Airborne beret. Tenderly he touched the flag. He stood at one end and inched closer to the opposite end of the bier. He simply stood there. And he wept. After a few minutes, he turned and hugged the young girlfriend of the hero. The fallen's father approached him, and they embraced. Twice the father told the young soldier, "He was doing what he wanted to do." The world was muted for a moment. Fresh tears fell for the sacrifice.

~~~~~~

John 11:33-35 on the occasion of the death of Lazarus, a dear friend of Jesus~~

"When Jesus saw Mary weeping, and the Jews who had come along with her also weeping, He was deeply moved in spirit and troubled. 'Where have you laid him?' He asked.
Come and see, Lord, they replied.
Jesus wept."

Sorry…but I just wasn't listening to you, world.
And in this muted moment, I remember Jesus' words…

~~*"I am the resurrection and the life. He who believes in me will live, even though he dies; and whoever lives and believes in me will never die. Do you believe this?"*
~~"Come to me, all you who are weary and burdened, and I will give you rest." Matthew 11:28

Written in honor and memory of Sgt. Keith Allen "Rabbit" Kline, Oak Harbor, Ohio
1983 - 2007

Sunday, July 15, 2007

May 24, 2007

The summer of his second deployment has arrived. He will have spent all the major holidays in this foreign country at the end of his term. So many of our sons and daughters are over in these foreign lands in President Bush's troop surge. I'm on vacation as I write these words. My son—our sons and daughters—will receive no vacation this summer of 2007. I watch the TV and hear them speak of a bloody August as a timetable is hatcheted around by the politicians.

I look at my husband and shake my head as I hear the growing arguments of ending the war and bringing the troops home. No one wants their son or daughter, husband or wife, home more than these military families. But the amazing thing that astounds me again and again is that these troops stand ready to die to defend the rights of those who vocalize the loudest. It is their duty and their highest calling to defend the Constitution of the United States. So be it Rosie O'Donnell or Elisabeth Hasselbeck, the troops defend their rights to freedom of speech and all the other liberties this land of freedom enjoys.

So many have paid the ultimate price for our liberties. Today at an art gallery in Sedona, Arizona, I was stopped in my tracks over a beautiful life size bronze statue. It was a World War II veteran, holding a flag in one hand and two bronzed poppies in the other. He was leaning forward on his bench, his hands resting upon a cane. On his chest were three medals: a Purple Heart, Bronze Star, and a

Blue Star In My Window

WWII medal. Over his hunched shoulders was cast an Army dress coat; and on his head a covering that read "USS Arizona." It could have been my Dad. I slipped my hands over the bony hands of the statue. I looked into the eyes of the World War II veteran who longed to see the ceasing of another war to end all wars. December 7, 1941 came and we vowed never to forget Pearl Harbor. Normandy D-Day, Omaha Beach, Pointe du Hoc where steep cliffs were scaled by brave Army Rangers. June 6, 1944. Have we forgotten? What sacrifice! What a price they paid. Korea. Never forget. Viet Nam. Never forget. Gulf War I. September 11. Never forget. Iraq. Have we forgotten again?

Links of the chain from foreign wars before this one of which we as a nation have grown weary. Links of the chain from one generation who believed in honor, courage, and commitment to the next. Nothing has changed in this regard. Each generation will answer a call to a greater good. World Wars I and II, Korea, Viet Nam, Persian Gulf, Iraq…all dot our recent history. How many more wars yet to come?

The wisest man who ever lived was King Solomon. And he wrote in ***Ecclesiastes 1:4 and 11: "Generations come and generations go…There is no remembrance of men of old, and even those who are yet to come will not be remembered by those who follow."***

I found a diary my mother kept as a young teen girl from 1938 to 1944. Notes about school and friends…names vaguely familiar to me. My mother, Helen, and my grandmother, Velta, must have shared the diary at times. In my grandmother's handwriting on this journal, I found this notation of my Uncle Bob: "Bobbie left home the 18th of November for Peoria. Left Peoria the 19th to Chicago in 1943." Uncle Bob's address then written in Grandma's script:

Prvt. Robert Lutes, Platoon 1080, R.D.M.C.B., San Diego 41, Calif." It was then followed by Prvt. Robert I. Lutes, 52nd Replacement Bn., Camp Pendleton, Ocean Side, Calif. And then one last note on May 11, 1944 (approximately 1 month prior to D-Day) in Grandma's handwriting: "Received word that Bobbie arrived overseas safely. Pvt. Robert I. Lutes, USMC, Company C, Replacement Bn. Marine Administration, II Marine Amphibious Corps., Forward Echelon, c/o Fleet P.O., San Francisco, Calif. Following that are so many names of young neighbors that were found in the back of Mom's diary:

Elvin Shurts, USS Yorktown
Prvt. Waldo K. Robinson, New York City, NY
Prvt. Thomas I. Coyne, US Army
Prvt. William Schultz
Prvt. F. C. Lawrence R. Wabel, San Francisco
Harold Wilkins; Beaufort, South Carolina
Prvt. Robert I. Bush, Recruiting Detachment, Randolph Field, TX
Prvt. Kirby Chapman, Hq. Sqd. 100th Air Base, Dale Mabry Field, Tallahassee, Florida.

I heard Mom mention some of these names. The boys from Henry, Illinois now deployed around the other side of the world, along with my sweet Uncle Bob. That greatest generation with post office boxes and names and faces of dearly loved family and friends shipping off to war. Prayers from Franklin D. Roosevelt in the Oval Office on June 6, 1944, as well as families at home.

Links in the chain.

A baton passed to another generation in a jungle. Draft notices and teenage boys again slipped away. Questions and dark discussions, cynicism. Prayers still go on. But darkness hovers. Questions of "Is God Dead?" in a pop culture where authority is protested. Still honor, courage, and commitment bear their marks on another generation of warriors and vows of Never Forget the sacrifice of POWs and MIAs are stifled in these turbulent years.

Still we prayed.
A link in the chain.

Turmoil in the Middle East.
October 23, 1983 Beirut, Lebanon and 241 U.S. Marines and sailors on a peacekeeping mission from Camp Lejeune are killed by a suicide bomber.
Courage. Honor. Commitment.
Nothing will change in that regard from that sandy place of deep resolve.
A link in the chain.
Persian Gulf War. Operation Iraqi Freedom.

Iraq Invasion. Operation Enduring Iraqi Freedom.

More prayers.

Sixty years later, another mother's diary full of addresses of soldiers and marines. A mother's scribbled notes of her son's whereabouts as he heads off to war in 2004.

One more blue star in the window.

Many, many more prayers.
A link in the chain.

The adversary has called for a jihad against our nation. The declaration of war began on September 11, 2001. In much the same way as the bombs fell on Pearl Harbor and the young men faced an enemy willing to commit suicide for their beliefs, our young troops face an adversary with no fear of death. This enemy of terror has declared this holy war against all infidels who do not bow and adhere to their Allah. Bringing our troops home will not signal an end to this jihad. It is only a sign post on the way to an ultimate battle.

Jesus' own words tell us in John 16:2-4:

"...a time is coming when anyone who kills you will think he is offering a service to God. They will do such things because they have not known the

Father or me. I have told you this so that when the time comes you will remember that I warned you."

Brothers and sisters in Christ, God's Word has spoken. We also have sign posts along the way which direct and guide.

This is what the LORD says, "Stand at the crossroads and look; ask for the ancient paths, ask where the good way is, and walk in it, and you will find rest for your souls." Jeremiah 6:16

Much of our nation and our world have embraced ancient Babylon's spirit. Babylon is no longer one geographical hot spot on our globe. It is a lifestyle of excess, pleasure, hedonism, and searching for an ultimate inner knowledge of one's being. We who are in Christ have a higher calling. And yet we dabble in the Babylonian community as well. God, help us.

Daniel of ancient Babylon recorded a telling message to those of a future *"time, times, and half a time. When the power of the holy people has been finally broken, all these things will be completed. I heard but I did not understand. So I asked, 'My lord, what will the outcome of all this be?' He replied, 'Go your way, Daniel, because the words are closed up and sealed until the time of the end. Many will be purified, made spotless and refined, but the wicked will continue to be wicked. None of the wicked will understand, but those who are wise will understand." Daniel 12:7-10*

I am neither a politician nor a great thinker.
I am simply a link in the chain of mankind.

And when I look back, I see the Hand of God as the ONLY constant that was always there. Courage, honor, and commitment—yes, that was certainly woven through the years from our finest young men and women.

But in the end, Jehovah God is the final Warrior left standing in the battle and this holy war for which the jihadists have called. And He is mounted on a white horse.

"I saw heaven standing open and there before me was a white horse, whose rider is called Faithful and True. With justice he judges and makes war. His eyes are like blazing fire, and on his head are many crowns. He has a name written on him that no one knows but he himself. He is dressed in a robe dipped in blood, and his name is the Word of God." Revelation 19:11-13

He is the Alpha and Omega, the First and the Last, the Beginning and the End. He is the Root and the Offspring of David, and the bright Morning Star.

He is the Prince of Peace: Jesus Christ, the son of the most High Jehovah.

And He is coming soon.

"Behold, I am coming soon! Blessed is he who keeps the words of the prophecy in this book." Revelation 22:7

WILL NOT THE JUDGE OF THE EARTH DO RIGHT?
GENESIS 18:25

THE INVITATION

Dear Warrior,

If you have come this far with me, thank you. We live in a far different world than that into which we were born. The times today are unsettling. We try to cover up the scariness and terror that seems to lurk on the edge of life with our high priced toys or fast paced lives. Yet that seems not to satisfy fully. We lull ourselves to sleep with our pills or pillow tunes, but awaken to the starkness of the darkness of our lives. We are tired of the lies. We seek truth. It's an age-old question echoed through Pilate's question to Jesus, "What is truth?" (John 18:38) Jesus tells us the truth. The Scriptures show Jesus saying over and over, "I tell you the truth…" I would be remiss not to point you, dear reader, to Jesus.

John 14:6 Jesus answered, "I am the way and the truth and the life. No one comes to the Father except through me."

He is the ONLY WAY.

In the book of Matthew, the Scriptures tell us Jesus was astounded by a military man…a Roman centurion. How do you astonish the Son of God?

Matthew 8:5-10

When Jesus had entered Capernaum, a centurion came to him, asking for help. "Lord," he said, "my servant lies at home paralyzed and in terrible suffering."

Jesus said to him, "I will go and heal him."

The centurion replied, "Lord, I do not deserve to have you come under my roof. But just say the word, and my servant will be healed. For I myself am a man under authority, with soldiers under me. I tell this one, 'Go,' and he goes; and that one, 'Come,' and he comes. I say to my servant, 'Do this,' and he does it."

When Jesus heard this, he was astonished and said to those following him, "I tell you the truth, I have not found anyone in Israel with such great faith. … Then Jesus said to the centurion, "Go! It will be done just as you believed it would." And his servant was healed at that very hour."

Without the faith of the no-nonsense, truth-seeking centurion in this modern day, much of this Iraq war makes little sense. In God's eternal frame of reference, eternity will answer the questions of today. That takes centurion faith. 100 x 100 x 100 x 100 multiplied-kind of faith. Without centurion faith that can astound ourselves and our world, this current conflict all becomes a disaster of missteps, mistakes, and misfortunes. Most of the world only sees greed for oil, money, power, and destroyed lives. But make no mistake, God is in sovereign control. He continues to move though history...His Story. Oh, God, give us the faith of a centurion that trusts, hopes, believes You can do what You said in Your Word. Thy Kingdom come, Thy will be done on earth as it is in heaven.

Jesus can come to you in the same way, modern centurion. If you found your faith forged in your journey borne through military service, that faith that has been your bedrock that you clung to in tough times, that faith in the living Son of God, will save you. And if you don't know Him, you can too. Booze, pills, drugs, pornography, suicide...many seek to pour these kinds of salve over their wounds and hope to simply forget. There is another way. Jesus waits. Come to Him.

Isaiah 55:6, 7

Seek the Lord while he may be found;
   Call on him while he is near.
Let the wicked forsake his way
   And the evil man his thoughts.
Let him turn to the Lord, and he will have mercy
   on him,
   And to our God, for he will freely pardon.

I'm not witty enough with words to debate you or convince you with intellectual prowess. Others have done that before far better than I. I am only a witness of His revealed glory. I only have known His comfort in valleys of shadows. I have met Him and know that He is the Master of any storm of life.

Come to Him. Receive Jesus.
   Call on Him while there is time.
      Read His Word.
         Build your house on the solid rock.

September 17, 2007

Last spring during a trip from Columbus to Toledo, we came upon an overpass. I didn't even notice it in the passing countryside. My son turned around and looked at it for a time then quietly said, "That reminds me of an overpass in Fallujah." He was silent for awhile as he turned it over in his mind.

There is so much emphasis currently on bringing the troops home. The swing of the opinion pendulum polls from the far left in MoveOn.org to the far right with the Moral Majority drive the news shows and media pundits. It's a political year. We're going to be hammered until November 2008 with fingers pointed at each other over the hot topic of the Iraq war and the troops. I'm already sick of it; and we still have more than a year of this to endure. I think it terribly wrong to call a highly decorated, honorable Bronze Star General a betrayer. He deserves our applause for

Blue Star In My Window

the job he has done—not scorn and ridicule in the press. I turn all this over in my mind also.

My son will soon return from his second deployment in Iraq. His time is almost over in this surge that President Bush called for in January 2007. His battalion will be coming back soon. They have accomplished much of which to be proud in Fallujah. Yet I know personally of so many more that are either over there right now or on their way shortly to Iraq or Afghanistan. They aren't nameless troops. They have nicknames, wives, fiancés, sweet children, Moms and Dads, homes in my community, and lives they've put on hold for their crucible in the desert.

When they do return home, most of them return quietly. We hardly even notice they're here. They blend in, grow their hair a bit or forget to shave for a time, pull out their favorite shirt and cargo pants and blend in. They'll drive their cars a little faster, play the music a little louder, go back to their jobs, and remember the gals and guys still over there. They'll see something over here that reminds them of over there. They'll remember the ones who didn't make it out alive. They'll think of the families of the fallen and want these families to know it was an honor to serve with their hero. Some of them will wrestle and fight on this side of the ocean with the stress of what they've endured. Too many will relearn to physically walk again or move with parts of their body now missing. They've endured grievous injuries. Some will endure them internally on their hearts and souls. No matter what your opinion is of the war, we have a generation of young warriors who have grown up in the desert. They left our shores and found or lost themselves in this sandbox. Their hands will help shape our American future.

So much of this current generation in the United States is mesmerized with their image. Everyone wants their five minutes of fame and seems to have found it in You Tube. It's all surface and slick gloss. We parents have spoiled and indulged this My Space generation even beyond what our parents did for us. (And our Baby Boom generation certainly did our share of being spoiled brats too!) What kind of depth comes from slick gloss though? How long before it wears thin?

These returning troops have had to endure the bleak desert. They've stood in the sandstorms, seen devastation, learned to go without and put life on hold. They've learned discipline, courage, patience, and have dealt with pain, anger, fatigue, and boredom. They've seen justice and injustice. They've given up a lot to complete their missions. They want the mission to count for something. They especially want the noble sacrifices made to mean something which will last for those fallen warriors who gave all. They can indeed be proud of their mission accomplishments the rest of their lives. These crucibles will count for something. Gold and silver will emerge from the trials faced and fought by these warriors.

Proverbs 17:3 *'The crucible for silver and the furnace for gold, but the LORD tests the heart."*

My wise sister Paula sent this quote to her nephew Kenton back in 1999. It was taken from Helen Keller; and because Kurt was born on the date of Helen Keller's birthday and also lost his eyesight, Helen Keller has always been a hero in our family. I pulled out the quote from this wonderful woman who battled life in her own way and came out a victor. I find her words still beautifully true for these warriors and the trial they have come through in this war.

"Character cannot be developed in ease and quiet. Only through experiences of trial and suffering can the soul be strengthened, vision cleared, ambition inspired and success achieved. Face your deficiencies and acknowledge them, but do not let them master you. The marvelous richness of human experience would lose something of rewarding joy if there were no limitations to overcome." Helen Keller

Captain Dave Pinion, USMC Commanding Officer of Echo Company in my son's first deployment 2005/2006 had a saying, "To those who fight for it, life has a special flavor that the protected will never know."

In the New Testament we find James' words in the first chapter, verses 2-4: *"Consider it pure joy, my brothers, whenever you face trials of many kinds, because you know that the testing of your faith develops perseverance. Perseverance must finish its work so that you may be mature and complete, not lacking anything."*

Many believe this war was fought simply because of oil. I'd like to possibly agree with this statement. Only it is not the oil found deep in the world's reserves in the Middle East. It may just be that the oil, often referred to in the Holy Bible as sacred, anointed oil, is to be poured out on all mankind…this soothing and sacred oil of God's Word that is so precious to any follower of Jesus Christ and is that Holy Spirit anointed oil of the good news of Jesus Christ. Jesus reveals much about this in Matthew 24: *"And this gospel of the kingdom will be preached in the whole world as a testimony to all nations, and then the end will come."*

The good news of Jesus Christ has been banned in Muslim countries for many years. Now it has found entrance through many of the troops and faithful, strong Christians in this desert land. Genesis traces back to the Tigris and Euphrates Rivers…life's origins. The gospel of the kingdom has reached some Muslim hearts, and God is showing His grace for these beloved descendants of Abraham and Ishmael. God will have His way in history.

I have passed Marine vans many times on the highway and noticed the picture of the Marines in the dress blue uniforms with the beautiful hand-polished, stainless steel sword and the phrase:

Earned. Never given.

Well, I would like to reverse that order to fit what God has done through His son Jesus Christ:

Given. Never earned.

as shown in John 3:16, 17: *"For God so loved the world that he gave his one and only Son that whoever believes in him shall not perish but have eternal life. For God did not send his Son into the world to condemn the world but to save the world through him."*

That sword, the Word of God, shows us there is nothing we can do. Isaiah 64:6 *"All of us have become like one who is unclean, and all our righteous acts are like filthy rags."* He has done it all for us as a free gift. It is truly Never Earned, Always Given. It is ours to simply receive.

Yet, O LORD, you are our Father.
  We are the clay, you are the potter;
  We are all the work of Your hand."
   Isaiah 64:8

Thank you for your service to our country and world, returning military troops. God will take your sacrifice and the work of your hand. He will use it to His glory in His own mysterious way.

For history is His story.

RESOURCES

Grateful acknowledgment is made to the following:

Brokow, Tom, **The Greatest Generation**. New York: Random House, 1998.

Cash, Johnny, "*American IV: The Man Comes Around*" album. Nashville: American Recordings LLC, 2002.

DeBoer, Roberta, "*A Family Sends A Son To War*," *The Blade*, Toledo, Ohio, September 25, 2005.

DeBoer, Roberta, "*From the Front, to the Laundry Room, and Back*," *The Blade*, Toledo, Ohio, Blog from February 22, 2007.

Keller, Helen. (1880 – 1968)

Lucado, Max, **No Wonder They Call Him The Savior: Experiencing the Truth of the Cross**. Nashville: W Publishing Group, a division of Thomas Nelson, Inc., 1986.

Moore, Beth, **Believing God**, Nashville: LifeWay Press, 2002.

Moore, Beth, **The Patriarchs: Encountering The God of Abraham, Isaac, and Jacob**, Nashville: LifeWay Press, 2005.

Newton, John, Lyrics of *Amazing Grace*/Music Carrell and Clayton's Virginia Harmony, 1831.

Norton, Paul, USMC 68-69, *The Agent* copywrited poem, Toledo, Ohio.

Schaeffer, Frank, **Keeping Faith: A Father Son Story About Love and the USMC**. New York: Carroll & Graf, 2002.

Scott, Tony, *Sermon notes*, Cathedral of Praise, the church on strayer.com, Maumee, Ohio.

Stone Jr., Perry, *Voice of Evangelism, Inc.*, P.O. Box 3595, Cleveland, Tennessee.

Swindoll, Charles R., **Bedtime Blessings**. Nashville: J Countryman, a division of Thomas Nelson, Inc., 2002.

Swindoll, Charles R. "*Insight For Living*" radio broadcasts, Plano, Texas.

West, Bing, **No True Glory A Frontline Account of the Battle For Fallujah**. New York: Bantam Dell A Division of Random House, Inc., 2005.

Yellowcard, "*Lights and Sounds*" album, "Two Weeks From Twenty." Capitol Records: January 24, 2006.

AUTOBIOGRAPHY

Catherine DePew is a 1975 graduate of Lincoln Christian College in Lincoln, Illinois. She has been employed by Nabisco/Kraft Foods for 25 years. She is a member of Cathedral of Praise in Maumee, Ohio and has been involved in children's ministry, facilitating Beth Moore women's Bible studies, and she and her husband are co-directors of Everyday Heroes Military Ministry. She is a member of the Northwest Ohio Marine Family Support Community. Her highest calling is that of a wife to Lenny and mother to Katelyn, Kenton, and daughter-in-law Julie. Cathy's newest joy is becoming a grandmother to Christian Kurt Dial.

Cathy enjoys the beauty of quilts, sunsets and sunrises, and the stars in the nighttime sky. She loves the Scriptures, aims to be a Proverbs 31 kind of gal, enjoys the friends she's made along the way (especially the 'yoyo sisterhood' from LCC), and loves a good garage sale!

Printed in the United States
200751BV00001B/118-525/A